Why Work?
Called to Make a Difference

Nancy D. Olsen and Howard W. Olsen, Ph.D.

Why Work?
Called to Make a Difference

© Copyright 2006 by M3 Planning, Inc.

All Scripture quotations, unless indicated, are taken from the Holy Bible: New International Version ®· NIV®. Copyright © 1973, 1978, 1984 by International Bible Society.

Scripture quotation marked (NASB) are taken from the New American Standard Bible, © 1960, 1962, 1963, 1968, 1971, 1972, 1973, 1975, 1977, and 1994 by The Lockman Foundation, La Habra, CA.

Scripture quotations marked (NKJV) are taken from the Holy Bible, New King James Version. Copyright © 1982 by Thomas Nelson, Inc.

Scripture quotations marked (MSG) are taken from The Message, the New Testament in Contemporary English© 1993 by Eugene H. Peterson, published by NavPress, Colorado Springs, CO.

Scripture quotations marked (NLT) are taken from the Holy Bible, New Living Translation, copyright © 1996, 2004 by Tyndale House Publishers, Inc., Wheaton, IL.

Published by
M3 Planning, Inc.
P.O. Box 8021. Reno, NV 89507
Copyright © 2006 M3 Planning, Inc. All rights reserved.

ISBN: 978-0-9748343-7-5
Version 1.0, January 2006
Printed in the United States of America

Contact us at www.MyStrategicPlan.com/kingdom

About the Authors

Nancy D. Olsen

Nancy Olsen is the vice president of M3 Planning, Inc., a business development firm that specializes in helping organizations develop their strategy to accomplish their growth plans. Nancy holds an MS in Education, an MA in Theology, and an MBA in Management. Her expertise is much more than academic, however, as the owner of five small businesses and an entrepreneurial consulting practice. Nancy's desire is to equip organizations to strategically use their resources to impact the marketplace and transform nations.

Howard W. Olsen, Ph.D., CPA

Howard Olsen is the president of M3 Planning, Inc. Howard is an entrepreneur with more than 25 years of business experience. He holds a Ph.D. in marketing with an international emphasis and is a CPA. Additionally, he served as an assistant professor of marketing at the University of Nevada, Reno. Howard's desire is to equip business leaders with practical tools for making their businesses a pro-active platform for ministry.

Howard and Nancy's Workplace

M3 Planning powers **MyStrategicPlan.com, MyNonProfitPlan. com, and MyChurchPlan.com.** The sites are respectively designed for businesses, nonprofits, and churches. Each site offers practical and integrated web-based tools for developing a market-based strategic plan to focus and grow the organization. Howard and Nancy's books support the online process.

- *Strategic Planning Made Easy:™ A Practical Guide to Growth and Profitability*
- *Strategic Planning for Purpose and Profitability: A Biblical Approach*
- *Strategic Planning Made Easy™ for Nonprofit Organizations: A Practical Guide*

Acknowledgements

This book assimilates thoughts, ideas, and knowledge from many sources. Our primary value as the authors has been in choosing the focus and then integrating and presenting the material.

We would like to acknowledge our family, friends, and workplace associates who contributed to its development. We would especially like to acknowledge Steve Gardner, our editor, who greatly enhanced its quality.

Table of Contents

Foreword..1

What Is the Purpose of This Book? 3

How Can This Book Be Used Most Effectively? 5

The Perfect Job 6

CHAPTER 1: Finding Your Destiny 7

CHAPTER 2: You, the Church, the Kingdom of God,
the Marketplace, the City................................15

CHAPTER 3: Working in the Kingdom......................23

CHAPTER 4: Workplace Ministers and Church Ministers.......29

CHAPTER 5: Workplace Ministers..........................33

CHAPTER 6: The Calling....................................39

CHAPTER 7: The Anointing..................................45

CHAPTER 8: The Marketplace...............................51

CHAPTER 9: Transforming Cities and Nations 63

CHAPTER 10: Bringing in the Harvest 73

CHAPTER 11: Building the Kingdom 83

CHAPTER 12: Workplace Minister and Church Minister
Relationships: Challenges and Opportunities 89

CHAPTER 13: Equipping 103

CHAPTER 14: Setting Apart and Commissioning 111

CHAPTER 15: Supporting Ministry in the Workplace 115

CHAPTER 16: Laying the Foundation for Planning 125

CHAPTER 17: Plan for Workplace Transformation 139

References...147

Foreword

Why Work? Called to Make a Difference

The first two words of this title really struck me: Why work? Now, there's a great question.

I don't know why, but the first thing that popped into my mind is how closely work and love are related. Have you ever noticed how many characteristics the words "work" and "love" share?

They are both four-letter words we use all the time. They are both nouns and verbs, depending on how we use them in a sentence. And they both cover a wide variety of meanings and emotions. Some lucky people love work; others hate it.

The genius of this book is that it shows you not only how you can love to work but also how you can work to love. People who know me will tell you I'm a fanatic on this subject. I love to see the lights come on in people's eyes when they first understand that their work can be the world's greatest mission field—that through their work they can love people to Christ.

Marketplace ministers don't preach in the traditional sense; their "preaching" is a combination of attitude, excellence in work, sensitivity and compassion for coworkers. It is a "word fitly spoken" when the time is right. Their ability to see the lost and unlovely through the eyes of Christ, who died for them, sets them apart from "holier-than-thou" religious turn-offs. Their prayer-closet intercession for those around them bears fruit that only eternity will reveal.

How would you feel if the President of the United States invited you to his office for a private meeting? Imagine his Secret Service agents ushering you into the Oval Office, and the President asking you to take a seat. As you sit, you notice the agents taking their places near the door. But then the President says, "That's all right, guys. We need a few minutes alone."

After they leave, the President, almost in a whisper, thanks you for coming and says, "I have an extremely important mission that I want you to do. There are others I could call, but you are my first choice."

Still trying to recover from the shock, you would probably ask, "Why me? You don't even know me."

"Oh, yes I do," he says. "I know virtually everything about you, including why you are where you are now. It's not by chance that you work where you work. We needed you there. You've been hand-picked, placed and groomed for this mission. But the choice is yours. What do you say, can I count on you?"

Fantasy? Of course it is. The President isn't God. He couldn't begin to have that kind of knowledge or power.

But if you take the President out of the story and replace him with God, you don't have a fantasy at all. You have pure reality. That is an accurate picture of how God wants to deal with you if you have eyes to see it and ears to hear it.

Go ahead. Read the book. You've been called. Open your eyes and ears to what God has in store for you. It's the adventure for which you were created.

Kent Humphreys
President, Fellowship of Companies for Christ International

What Is the Purpose of This Book?

This book exists to help you better understand and fulfill your calling from God to make a difference in the marketplace through your work. It will heighten your awareness of *why* you work—a reason far greater than merely supplying your financial needs.

You will see your role in a divine strategy, a role that you can appreciate now although it will take eternity's continuing light to fully comprehend. As an agent of God to bring transformation to your workplace, you will see the people you encounter every day in a new way. You will rejoice at what God does through you as He changes their lives.

Whether your workplace is in corporate America, at home, or in the government, God can use you to transform your workplace, the marketplace, and the world. He wants you to be an integral part of bringing His Kingdom into every sphere of influence He opens to you.

We highlight work-related Scriptures that you can apply as you consider the Reflection and Discussion Questions in each chapter. Since we believe that God created all of life to glorify Himself and work out His purposes, we have designed this book to help you integrate rather than separate your work and spiritual life, tearing down the artificial wall between "sacred" and "secular."

In addition to more than fifteen years of personal experience, we have drawn heavily from current books on the topic and countless hours of discussions with marketplace Christians. We have endeavored to be succinct, honoring the time of our busy workplace colleagues. Each chapter is thought provoking and worthy of discussion, guiding everyday workers into supernatural workplace ministry.

How Can This Book Be Used Most Effectively?

The style and content of this book make it appropriate for multiple settings. Most people who are not employed as professional ministers suffer from confusion over their role in God's plan to redeem mankind. They have had little or no exposure to the concept of workplace ministry. Among the questions for which they need answers are:

- What is the biblical basis for workplace ministers?
- What are their responsibilities?
- What does it mean to bring the Kingdom of God into the workplace?

As valuable as this is for the individual reader, it is even more valuable when used in small groups, whether in the marketplace or in the local church. The Reflection and Discussion Questions at the end of each chapter encourage small-group discussion that enhances the understanding of all participants.

Some have chosen to use it as a textbook. Whether used in a small group setting or in a classroom, an outline summary of each chapter can be downloaded for group use from the website **www. MyStrategicPlan.com/kingdom - under "Books."**

Others have used this material as a reference for sermons as they embrace and address the workplace ministry concept. The church as a whole benefits as it gains a more comprehensive view of God's plan to speak to the world through the workplace.

The Perfect Job

- My first job was working in an orange juice factory, but I got canned…couldn't concentrate.
- After that I tried to be a tailor, but I just wasn't suited for it… mainly because it was a so-so job.
- Then I tried to be a chef—figured it would add a little spice to my life, but I just didn't have the thyme.
- Next I tried working in a muffler factory, but that was too exhausting.
- I managed to get a good job working for a pool maintenance company, but the work was just too draining.
- I attempted to be a deli worker, but any way I sliced it, I couldn't cut the mustard.
- Then I worked in the woods as a lumberjack, but I just couldn't hack it, so they gave me the axe.
- Next was a job in a shoe factory; I tried but I just didn't fit in. So then I got a job in a workout center, but they said I wasn't fit for the job.
- After many years of trying to find steady work I finally got a job as a historian until I realized there was no future in it.
- I studied a long time to become a doctor, but I didn't have any patience.
- My best job was being a musician, but eventually I found I wasn't noteworthy.
- I became a professional fisherman but discovered that I couldn't live on my net income.
- My last job was working at Starbucks, but I had to quit because it was always the same old grind.
- So I retired and found I'm perfect for the job!

(Source: www.whoohoo.net)

CHAPTER 1

FINDING YOUR DESTINY

Do not let your occupation block your destiny, but instead let your destiny shape your occupation by turning it into your ministry.
— *Ed Silvoso*

What do you know about your destiny? Have you given any significant thought to the possibility that destiny is not just a Hollywood concept — that when God uniquely designed you He had a plan? Understanding who you are and discovering God's call on your life are foundational for knowing how your work uniquely fulfills Kingdom purposes.

God's Purpose for Work and Its Place in God's Plans

God is accomplishing His plan and purpose through you. God is the master of mutually beneficial multitasking. Not only is He reclaiming His kingdom on earth—a kingdom temporarily usurped by Satan—but He is also providing redemption for mankind and creation. His plan guarantees victory over the counterfeit satanic kingdom while it simultaneously provides salvation for mankind. Christ's death on the cross established the groundwork for these two purposes to be accomplished. Through Christ's redemptive love, man can believe and be saved, experiencing dominion over the earth and victory over Satan's kingdom.

Work is good and has intrinsic value. Multiple biblical passages support this truth. First, in the opening chapters of Genesis we see God Himself working in His creation of both the universe and mankind. The focus of the entire Bible is God's continuing work to accomplish the redemption of both fallen man and His Kingdom.

A second indication that work is good is that God created man in His image as a worker and ruler. *"Then God said, 'Let us make man in our image, in our likeness, and let them rule over the fish of the sea and the birds of the air, over the livestock, over all the earth, and over all the creatures that move along the ground.' So God created man in his own image, in the image of God he created him; male and female he created them. God blessed them and said to them, 'Be fruitful and increase in number; fill the earth and subdue it. Rule over the fish of the sea and the birds of the air and over every living creature that moves on the ground'"* (Genesis 1:26-28).

Third, God directed Adam to work and care for the Garden. *"The Lord God took the man and put him in the Garden of Eden to work it and take care of it"* (Genesis 2:15). Note that this occurred before the Fall. God instituted work for man's benefit, not for his punishment.

Finally, work is a principal means of fulfilling the Great Commandments: to love God, to love other people, and to love yourself. God's purpose for your work flows out of these commandments. This is the essence of His will for you. Through work, God is using you to bless others by demonstrating His love. He first demonstrated His redemptive love to mankind through the sacrifice of Christ. Now He invites you to exemplify it as His ambassador through your relationships with others. *"We are therefore Christ's ambassadors, as though God were making his appeal through us"* (2 Corinthians 5:20).

Nature of Work

Work is productive activity, whether paid or unpaid. It includes expending energy to serve others in ways that benefit the community, glorify God, and fulfill the individual. Many stay-at-home parents, volunteers, and retired people provide valuable service for the Kingdom without receiving payment for their work.

The work you do is significant and matters to God. He created you for a specific role in His overall purpose of establishing His Kingdom on earth.

God invites you to be a coworker with Him in accomplishing this purpose. "For I am God's workmanship, created in Christ Jesus to do good works, which God prepared in advance for me to do" (Ephesians 2:10). God invites you to participate with Him in His Kingdom work. He accomplishes His work through the good works that He has prepared in advance for you to do.

Work is a gift God has given to you. It is an honor to participate with God in His work. He has divinely appointed tasks for you—tasks which not only glorify Him but also satisfy your needs as well. God's plan for work is a win-win situation.

Work is doing whatever God has called and motivated you to do. Instead of focusing on finding the "perfect" job, focus on identifying the passions God has given you. Biblical examples of workplace motivation are seen in the life of Joseph (Genesis 41:25-57) and the Apostle Paul. Our workplace motivation can be summed up by Jesus' words in John 17:4, *"I have brought you glory on earth by completing the work you gave me to do."*

God uses the workplace to transform your character. In order for God to use you, your character and faith must be Christ-like. God is transforming your character, motives, attitudes, and values so that you exemplify the redemptive power of Christ-like love in your work.

God's Pattern for Work and Rest

God models and calls us to a Sabbath rest. The second chapter of Genesis tells us that God rested on the seventh day from all the work He had done. He set the pattern for work and rest by His own example of performing the work of creation in six days and resting on the seventh. So important was this pattern for us to follow that God made it one of the Ten Commandments along with the prohibition against killing, dishonesty and idol worship.

The fourth commandment calls us to a Sabbath rest: *"Remember to observe the Sabbath day by keeping it holy. Six days a week are set apart for your daily duties and regular work, but the seventh day is a day of rest dedicated to the LORD your God"* (Exodus 20:8-10 NLT). The Sabbath rest is part of a larger, God-ordained pattern for our relationship to work. Its purpose is to empower and root our work in "being" rather than simply "doing" endless activity.

Sabbath means resting in the completed work of God. We trust God's sufficiency, having confidence that He will meet our needs and move us in accordance with His plan. We recognize that His plan is superior to ours and that it is in our best interest to fit in with it.

Sabbath is trusting in the completed work of the cross. To observe a Sabbath rest is to admit that our work alone will never be enough to sustain us. We are not self-sufficient; we need God's help. Observing a Sabbath rest testifies against the lie that our significance is measured by our achievements. It testifies in favor of the truth that Christ's work on the cross is complete regardless of our social status or the size of our bank account. Only His finished work can sustain us.

The believer's spiritual rest is in Christ. We were never meant to do life on our own. Our weariness tends to draw us into the presence of God. Jesus says, *"Come to Me, all you who labor and are heavy laden, and I will give you rest. Take My yoke upon you and learn from Me, for I am gentle and lowly in heart, and you will find rest for your souls. For My yoke is easy and My burden is light"* (Matthew 11:28-30 NKJV). We serve a living God through our work; by faith we lay hold of Christ's rest and enter into the enjoyment of the work-rest pattern.

Fulfilling Your Destiny in God's Plan

All of us have "callings" in the world. We each have a "calling" in our families (as husbands, wives, parents, children), in our society (as citizens), in our church (as pastors, elders, members), and in our work (as we use the gifts God has given us). We serve God in all of our work, not just in work that is specifically church-related. Colossians 3:23-24 commands, *"Whatever you do, work at it with all your heart, as working for the Lord, not for men, since you know that you will receive an inheritance from the Lord as a reward. It is the Lord Christ you are serving."* God has called each of us to specific tasks, relationships, and types of work in which we are to love and serve Him and our neighbors. In turn, God blesses our work as we faithfully live out our calling.

God has uniquely crafted you with certain abilities, interests, motivations and aspirations. He has wired you to experience the joy of using your special abilities, talents, and gifts to serve others while simultaneously accomplishing God's Kingdom purposes.

Work gives your life purpose and fulfillment. As you do the work God has uniquely designed you to do, your need for purpose in life is fulfilled. Your work enables you to provide for your own family, serve others through giving, and love God in a practical way. Accomplishing your unique God-given purpose gives you more joy, increased motivation, focus, and success in your work. In God's final evaluation of your life you will be able to answer honestly, "Yes, my life was used to serve you, Lord." And Jesus will say, "Well done my good and faithful servant."

You have the full power of heaven at your disposal to fulfill your divine destiny (See John 14:14 and Philippians 4:13). *"He who began a good work in you will carry it on to completion"* (Philippians 1:6). Strive to know the life mission God has established for you. Rely on His power to accomplish it, and do not despise small beginnings. For example:

- Jesus began as a carpenter and touched the lives of millions.
- David began as the shepherd of a small flock and became the shepherd of Israel.
- Peter began as a fisherman and became a premier fisher of men.

God wants to give you greater influence. Jesus often spoke about giving responsibility based on what we do with the little things first. We see an example of this in the Parable of the Talents (Matthew 25:14-30). God will enlarge a person's influence when He knows that person will use it wisely for the Kingdom. For example, God saw the heart of Jabez and gave him his request by enlarging his borders. Jabez knew what it meant to ask passionately for God's favor. 1 Chronicles 4:9-10 says, *"Jabez was more honorable than his brothers. His mother had named him Jabez, saying, 'I gave birth to him in pain.' Jabez cried out to the God of Israel, 'Oh, that you would bless me and enlarge my territory! Let your hand be with me, and keep me from harm so that I will be free from pain.' And God granted his request."*

Finding Your Life Purpose

The key to discovering your life purpose is to begin with God. It is God who has implanted dreams, ambitions, goals, and desires in your heart. Open it and invite God to narrow your focus on the core of your calling.

One way to clarify your life purpose is to work through a guided reflection sequence that looks at your past, present, and ideal future. Doug Fike, Executive Director of Growth Dynamics International, has developed an effective Life Focus process that begins with these steps.

- Look for the continuing threads that are woven throughout your life—circumstances, interests, themes, and patterns of behavior.
- Identify God's design in your life, discerning and embracing the clues to your unique identity.
- Take inventory by jotting down initial reflections in each of the following areas:

   Life circumstances – Examine my life circumstances, including difficult ones, which shaped me in fundamental ways. These may include circumstances that were beyond my control, such as where I was born, the generation I was a part of, my upbringing, birth order, economic status, and gender.

   Needs I am drawn to – What circumstances really tug at my heart? What kinds of situations have I responded to throughout my life? What problems in the world would I give my life to solve? What kinds of needs do I want to meet? What am I most passionate about? In what kinds of work experiences have I most strongly felt God's presence?

Experience and fruit – In what areas do I have valuable experience? What has it prepared me to do? What kinds of work have produced the best fruit? What have I learned about who I am and what I don't want to do from negative experiences?

Confirmation and counsel – What have others affirmed in me? What significant, resonating counsel or feedback have I gotten about what I should do? What activities or achievements have resulted in the greatest positive feedback? When do others say, "This is really you!"? Ask the people who know you best: "What do you see as my single greatest strength?"

Gifts, skills, abilities – What do I have a natural gift or talent to do? What important skills have I developed? In what kinds of situations do my abilities really stand out? What do I do exceptionally well? What are my spiritual gifts? What is my personality style or type? What do I know about myself from various self-assessment tests? (Valuable tests include DISC, Myers-Briggs, Keirsey Temperament, Taylor-Johnson Temperaments, C.A.R.E. Profile, Spiritual Gift tests, etc.)

Inner knowing – What do I think I've been called to do? What have I always wanted to do with my life, maybe since I was a kid? About what do I have a sense of destiny? What do I think I might be or do someday?

Fulfillment and delight – When did I do something that just "clicked," something I felt born to do? What have I accomplished that was especially fulfilling? What are the little things in life that give me great pleasure?

Revelation – In what ways do I sense that God has spoken to me about my life purpose? What key Scriptures have I sensed having something to do with my life purpose? What prayers have been spoken over me? What "calling" experiences have I had?

As you examine each area, look for patterns and threads that will give you insight into your life purpose. The Life Focus process integrates these insights into a larger convergence, incorporating dreams, values, and personal goal-setting. Trained life coaches are available through the Transformational Leadership Coaching organization (www.transformationalcoaching.com), to help guide you through the full Life Focus process. The Life Focus discovery process is also available to churches and organizations through a series of Destiny Discovery Quest seminars (contact info@growthdynamics.org for further information).

Reflection and Discussion

1. Have you considered that the devil may fear you as a workplace Christian? What are some ways he has tried to prevent you from fulfilling your divine destiny in your place of work?

2. Can God enlarge your territory and entrust you to use it for His purposes? Ask God today to enlarge your territory. Ask Him to make you the kind of man or woman who is worthy of such trust.

3. Do you trust that God's work is complete in your life even when your work is not complete? Do you trust that God's work is sufficient to sustain you even though your work is not sufficient?

4. Do you trust that God's work is sufficient to move you in accordance with His plan?

5. Have you observed a Sabbath this week?

CHAPTER 2

YOU, THE CHURCH, THE KINGDOM OF GOD, THE MARKETPLACE, THE CITY

To change a city you have to change the marketplace. To change the marketplace, it will take Christians in the marketplace.
— Ed Silvoso

Who are *you*? What is the *Church*? What is the *Kingdom* of God? What is the role of the *marketplace*? How does all of that relate to the *city*? We need a major paradigm shift to integrate these five elements. Our current mindset is: I am John Smith; I am a member of First Church; the Kingdom of God is when Jesus comes back to earth; the marketplace is an evil place; my city has so many problems that I am waiting for the new Jerusalem.

However, in order to move forward, it is vitally important that you, the Church, the Kingdom, the marketplace, and the city all be interconnected. Imagine someone giving you an engine, a transmission, a car frame, four wheels, and a steering mechanism and claiming that they had given you a car. These disconnected parts, as valuable as they might be, will not get you far. To establish the necessary connectivity, we will examine each of these elements.

Who Are You?

I am created by God, empowered by Jesus, and I have a destiny. Ephesians 2:10 says, *"For we are God's workmanship, created in Christ Jesus to do good works, which God prepared in advance for* us to do." The four main points of this verse are:

- I am God's workmanship.
- I am created in Christ Jesus.
- I am to do good works.
- These works were prepared beforehand by God Himself.

Jesus has given me the Great Commandment. Matthew 22:37-39 instructs, *"Love the Lord your God with all your heart and with all your soul and with all your mind…Love your neighbor as yourself."* This gives us a two-point agenda for good works:

1. I must love God.
2. I must love my neighbor as myself. I am to hate sin, but love the person.

Jesus has given me the Great Commission. Matthew 28:18-20 says, *"All authority in heaven and on earth has been given to me. Therefore go and make disciples of all nations, baptizing them in the name of the Father and of the Son and of the Holy Spirit, and teaching them to obey everything I have commanded you."* All the power of Jesus is available for me.

What Is the Church?

Church (ekklesia) is "the assembly of the called." The Church consists of those who have been "called out." The word *ekklesia* is derived from two Greek words: *ek*, meaning "out" and *kaleo*, meaning, "call." The Church is composed of people "called out" of the world and into the Kingdom of God. This calling out is not from ordinary responsibilities but from slavery to sin and evil. The Church, by definition, consists of all who have been called out of the world, delivered, saved, and sanctified.

The Church is composed of individuals corporately united in Jesus Christ coming together in assembly. Whenever believers gather in Jesus' name—whether many or only two or three— Church is in session.

The Church is composed of people who carry the Kingdom with

16

them wherever they go. Jesus said, *"The Kingdom of God is within you"* (Luke 17:21). It is men and women, masters and slaves, parents and children—who have acknowledged Jesus as their Lord and Savior. They have been set free from the kingdom of darkness and transferred to the Kingdom of light.

The Church is commissioned to bring the Kingdom of God to earth. Jesus told us to pray, *"Your Kingdom come, your will be done on earth as it is in heaven"* (Matthew 6:10). The Church influences society as it lives out Kingdom principles and values in every arena of life.

The Church is to be dynamic and expansive rather than confined to four walls. The focus of the Church has been on bringing people into a church building instead of taking the Kingdom to the people. Believers have been urged to invite sinners to their services to hear a preacher tell them how to receive the Lord.

Jesus, however, presented the Kingdom of God not as something that people need to be brought into but as something that comes near to them. Jesus said, *"The Kingdom of God has come near to you"* (Luke 10:9). In fact, the most dramatic power encounters recorded in the books of Acts didn't happen until the disciples finally left Jerusalem 14 years after Jesus' clear admonition (Acts chapters 8-12). This demonstrated God's wisdom and direction for going to the lost rather than waiting for them to come.

Likewise, the Church today needs to go to the people and minister to them. The biblical word for "ministry" is *diakonia,* which means "service." Service can be seen biblically as "ministry." This means that the saints can do the work of the ministry—not just in the *nuclear* local church, but in the *extended* church as well. Members of a congregation are already strategically placed during the week in workplaces, neighborhoods, and campuses all over the city. A good example is this Ecclesiastic Lockout Story.

> *Richard Gazowsky, the pastor of Voice of Pentecost, in San Francisco, California, realized some time ago that his members were somehow confused on this issue. Worse yet, he believed, the pride they felt in coming to church—that is,*

to the church building—in such a godless city made them too "religious." Gazowsky decided to do something drastic about the situation. Richard put his parishioners on a 40-day "church-building fast"—he instructed them not to come to the church building for 40 days. If they did, they would find the doors locked.

During this unusual fast, members were asked not to spend time with other Christians or listen to Christian radio or TV or read Christian magazines; instead they were instructed to invest time in befriending neighbors and going to sporting and social events with them. In addition, every week when the members stopped by the church office to bring their tithes and offerings, Richard gave them a map showing a section of the city where they were to place doorknob hangers displaying this message: "God loves you and so do we. If you need prayer, contact our church at this phone number. If you come by, we will gladly give you a Bible."

The goal was to make contact with every home in San Francisco. Minutes away from midnight on the 40th day, in the midst of a fierce storm, the last home in the city was contacted, bringing the total to about 261,900. The results were extraordinary: 8,600 people called for prayer, 10,000 Bibles were given away, 4,100 inquired about salvation and 150 were baptized immediately. And this happened in San Francisco, of all places! Richard proved that when we move the picnic outdoors, everybody wants to join in!
(Silvoso, Ed. *"The Church Was Not Born in the Upper Room."* www. hischurchatwork.com).

What Is the Kingdom of God?

Jesus used the word "Church" only three times and "Kingdom" 78 times. Ironically, we know so much about church and so little about Kingdom. What is the Kingdom of God and how does it relate to the workplace?

The Kingdom of God refers to God's rule or reign—His kingship, His sovereignty. It is present, everlasting, universal, and is to be established. The Kingdom of God is both present and imminent. It is "already" and "not yet." The Kingdom is "already" because the rule of God is present in Jesus, but it is "not yet" in its full manifestation. The Kingdom, the new order of God, has already come in Jesus Christ, in his incarnation, his death and resurrection. The signs of the Kingdom are presently here as experienced in the gifts and the fruits of the Spirit, in its struggles against the flesh, the world, sin, and the powers of darkness. The Kingdom will come fully with the final coming of the Lord.

The Church lives in tension between the kingdom of "this age" and "the age to come." This age is one marked by evil, Satan's rule, and anxiety. The age to come is one of righteousness, joy, fellowship, eternal life, salvation, resurrection, and new creation. The Church in the present age represents the age to come.

The keys to the Kingdom are given to the Church. Jesus connected the word "Church" to the Kingdom. *"You are Peter, and upon this rock I will build My church; and the gates of Hades shall not overpower it. I will give you the keys of the kingdom of heaven; and whatever you shall bind on earth shall be bound in heaven, and whatever you shall loose on earth shall be loosed in heaven"* (Matthew 16:18-19). We draw two basic truths from these verses: First, the gates of hell shall not prevail against the Church. When believers come together in the workplace, the gates of hell will not prevail. Second, the Church has the power to bind and release on earth and in heaven.

Bringing the Kingdom into the workplace can transform its environment and conditions. The Church is comprised of believers who can bring the Kingdom of God to confront the kingdom of darkness in their workplace. The Kingdom of God represents light, organization, peace, order, love, honesty, righteousness, and joy.

What Is the Role of the Marketplace?

Marketplace refers to everything that is happening in the city. It refers to all areas of work: family life, school activities, entertainment, recreation, arts, government, education, and business. The marketplace is the life of the city.

The Kingdom of God operates in the marketplace. God's people in the various marketplace arenas are the key to making a difference. They have influence over their sphere of work. The Church is the light of the world and the salt of the earth. Christians can bring transformation to the marketplace by appropriating their power and authority in Christ over the kingdom of darkness.

Christians in their place of work have a role to play in healing the land and bringing about reconciliation. The Bible says, *"If my people humble themselves and pray and seek my face after turning from their wicked ways, I will hear their prayers, will forgive their sin and I will heal the land"* (2 Chronicles 7:14). The economy sustains everything that emanates from the land, all of which has been defiled by sin. Many Christians are operating their companies in a substandard manner because they are copying the best-demonstrated practices of non-Christian companies.

Businesses need reconciliation. Reconciliation is bringing into unity, harmony, or agreement that which has been alienated due to human sin. The Greek work for reconciliation, *katallage*, means "to enhance and increase the value of someone else." God has saved us to add value to others. We need to ask ourselves, "How can I add value to others? How can I as a mature person make adjustments for those who are weaker because of our differences?"

How Does This Play out in the City?

When you change the marketplace, you change the city. The ultimate objective is to bring transformation to the city. The Great Commission begins with the city and it will end when the last city is reached. For this to happen, the marketplace must be transformed.

The key is integrating you, the Church, the Kingdom of God, the marketplace, and the city. We are called to minister to the city, not just to a local church congregation. Here is a brief recap of this chapter's main points.

- *You* are God's workmanship, created in Christ to do good works. You are the salt of the earth and the light on a hill.

- You are the *Church*. You are not just an individual but a member of the Church. When you connect with another believer, Church is in session.

- The Church brings the *Kingdom of God* to confront the kingdom of darkness wherever it has been established. You can push back the kingdom of darkness by bringing in the Kingdom of light.

- The Kingdom of God operates in the *marketplace*. You can bring transformation to your place of work by using your power and authority in Christ.

- When you change the marketplace, you change the *city*.

Reflection and Discussion

1. How has Satan's deception affected your understanding of the Kingdom of God, the nature of the Church, and the Church's role in the marketplace?

2. Why is the idea that the Church is to operate within the four walls of a local assembly detrimental to our identity and our role in the Kingdom?

3. What would it mean for you to take the Kingdom of God to the people in your workplace?

4. What would it mean for you to have church in your workplace? What obstacles might you face in this endeavor?

CHAPTER 3

WORKING IN THE KINGDOM

*God has begun an evangelistic movement in the workplace that
has the potential to transform our society as we know it.*
— *Franklin Graham*

To what extent do you view your work as working in the
Kingdom? We have a God-given desire to make a difference in the
world—a difference of eternal significance. Many of us, however,
fail to see how we can do that in the place where we work. This
chapter supplies some missing links as we catch a glimpse of God's
perspective.

Work Is Worship

God sees our work as worship. The Hebrew word *avodah* is the
root word from which we get the words "work" and "worship." Work
is mentioned more than 800 times in the Bible. The word "work" is
even used to express a combination of worship, music, praise, and
singing. Work in the Bible is never presented as a non-spiritual pursuit;
our work is as spiritual as worshipping God in church.

We are to work and take care of God's creation. In the Garden
of Eden, labor was worship. When Adam and Eve took care of the
garden, they were worshipping, serving and honoring God. Likewise
today, when you go to work, you take care of God's garden, His
creation. You work in God's garden to produce plentiful fruit.

*We are to redeem mankind and creation. We are to destroy Satan's
kingdom and set the captives free.* Redemption refers to deliverance

from bondage, a release of someone or something from an alien power that has a claim upon it. That alien claim can be lifted only when one who has the right to do so acts to effect this release. After the Fall of mankind, Jesus' strategy was two-fold. As God's representatives, we are to:

1. Redeem mankind and creation. The entire creation was lost, not just individual souls. With Adam and Eve's first sin, Satan contaminated the totality of creation. Jesus, the perfect sacrifice, paid the price of redemption with His own blood. He broke the condemning power of the first sin by bringing redemption to mankind and creation.

2. Destroy Satan's kingdom and set captives free. In Jesus' first recorded sermon, he said that He came *"to preach good news to the poor…to proclaim freedom for the prisoners and recovery of sight for the blind, to release the oppressed"* (Luke 4:18). He launched the Church, which He commissioned to proclaim that freedom (Matthew 16:18-19).

We are to reclaim, redeem, and restore people and the land by working in God's Garden. As God's workers, we have been given a mandate to *"Be fruitful and increase in number; fill the earth and subdue it. Rule over the fish of the sea and the birds of the air and over every living creature that moves on the ground"* (Genesis 1:28).

Each of us has a part to play in this reclaiming, redeeming, and restoring. We have all been called to work in God's Garden. It encompasses all professions. Our job is to recapture the sacredness of our work, recognizing that it involves restoring people and redeeming the land from the curse. We are to drive the snake out of the land through intercession and our work, which is an expression of worship. Each of us needs to ask, "How can I redeem from the curse the people and the ground where I work?"

As Christians, we have been given authority over domains in our society. All the domains in our society are God's. Based on Genesis 1:28, we have been given a dominion mandate to subdue the earth and "rule…over every living creature…" The marketplace is an area where transformation can take place because of those who are in authority. If every believer would go to work fully convinced that he or she is worshiping God through labor and that every constructive action at work is a form of caring for God's creation, our cities would never be the same.

Sacred-Secular Dichotomy

A biblical worldview leaves no room for sacred-secular, dualistic thinking. The God of the Bible is actively involved in His world and engaged with His creation. As previously mentioned, the Hebrew word *avodah* is the root word from which we get the words "work" and "worship." God sees our work as worship.

The first-century Christians had an integrated lifestyle of work and ministry. They had no concept of a sacred-secular divide — the sense that our "faith life" is separate from our "work life."

Today, many people segregate work into either sacred or secular categories. This view maintains a hierarchy of sacred religious activities over secular demands and pursuits, including work, creating a constant tension between them. The view claims that sacred work — prayer, worship, church activities, evangelism, and ministry — deals with the eternal and is truly the work that matters to God. On the other hand, secular work such as jobs, hobbies, politics, and errands contribute nothing to God's work and exist only to meet the survival needs of man. It believes that secular work is not concerned with God and that it, in fact, takes away from the sacred categories.

This sacred-secular dichotomy is based on a faulty premise. The faulty premise says that God exists in a higher reality, a holy realm that we can enter only through the door of religion, and that any relationship with Him is separate from the rest of our lives. But this separation is not biblical. Additionally, this faulty view of work sees no inherent dignity or lasting value in everyday work.

If you are living with a divided sacred-secular worldview, you will tend to make one of two choices: You will separate yourself as much as possible from "worldly" things or you will forget God and devote yourself to the pursuit of success as the world defines it. Trying to live simultaneously in segregated worlds is confusing and crippling.

Strive to integrate sacred and secular work activities. As long as we continue to think that we are involved in secular work in the marketplace and sacred work in the church, we will continue to believe that there are two standards for living—one for work and another for church. If we believe that the work God has given us to do in the marketplace is less than the call given to professional religious people, we will never be what God designed us to be. Nor will the body of Christ be all it is intended to be.

The truth is that all of life relates to God. There is no distinction between sacred and secular in our relationship with Him. In everything we do, God is looking at our heart attitudes. His concern is that our motives be pure and righteous. God desires for all of our work to be brought in front of Him. He wants to be part of the daily chores of life as well as the decisions in our workplace. Since so much of our time is spent in the workplace, we must learn to integrate scriptural principles there. An important but neglected role of the church is to help us do this.

Working in God's Kingdom

The Gospel of Salvation is to be the full Gospel of the Kingdom. The Gospel of Salvation, like your birthday, is only the beginning of your life. The Gospel of the Kingdom incorporates all the days in your life. The introduction to the message is not the whole message. In fact, the bulk of the Old Testament is not about salvation; It is about how to disciple a nation of people in law, economics, science and technology. Jesus always referred to the Gospel as the Gospel of the Kingdom, not the Gospel of Salvation.

Having the "rights" to the Kingdom of God involves responsibilities. The Gospel of Salvation gives a person the *rights* to the promises of God. With the Gospel of the Kingdom come the *responsibilities* to live as part of the Kingdom. The Great Commission says we are to *"make disciples of all nations"* (Matthew 28:19). Part of how we disciple people is by bringing Kingdom principles such as justice, righteousness, mercy, and peace into our work environment. Our lives and work are to reflect the Gospel of the Kingdom.

There are eight Kingdom domains of influence. If we want to change a nation, we need to focus on the centers of influence and take scriptural principles into every one of them. We have identified the following eight Kingdom domains of influence: Church, Family, Government, Education, Arts, Communication, Science, and Business.

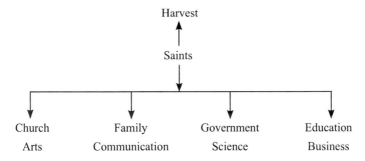

Notice the pivotal position of the saints in the diagram. As they bring the Gospel of the Kingdom into the eight domains of influence, they produce the fruit of harvest. God has specifically placed each of us for that reason, giving us influence and authority over our particular domain.

Reflection and Discussion

1. Do you see your work as an act of worship? Most likely when you come to a church meeting you feel spiritually higher than when you go to work because you have established the presence of God at church but not at work. If you were able to establish God's presence at work, you would feel a new spiritual depth and vitality there as well.

2. How does God's mandate to Adam and Even in the Garden apply to His mandate for you in the workplace?

3. Why have Christians believed that their place of work is less spiritual than church?

4. Do you feel your work outside the church is less spiritual than work inside the church?

5. How can you bring the Kingdom of God into your workplace?

6. What would your workplace look like if everyone were discipled?

7. Reflect on this quote: "Use now what God has given you, Count not its worth as small; God does not ask of you great things, Just faithfulness—that's all!" (Bosch)

CHAPTER 4

WORKPLACE MINISTERS AND CHURCH MINISTERS

God has made us kings and priests.
— Revelation 1:6 (NKJ)

For many years now, authors Larry Burkett, Doug Sherman, Dennis Peacocke and others have written books and articles on how to operate a business according to biblical principles. We have heard the call to become more proactive in demonstrating what it means to be a Christian in the workplace.

More recently, we see a growing awareness in the Church that more should be happening in the marketplace than simply being a Christian there or operating your business based on Christian principles. A trend, called workplace ministry or workplace transformation, is finally building momentum. In fact, during this past decade, the number of workplace-oriented ministries is growing at an exponential rate according to Os Hillman, director of the International Coalition of Workplace Ministries.

Workplace transformation is not a new concept. Throughout the Bible there are many examples of church and workplace ministers working together to fulfill God's purpose of redeeming mankind and building His Kingdom. God has called some people to serve in the church and others to serve in the city.

Two Callings

Revelation 1:6 says that God *"made us kings and priests"* (NKJV).

David High, who used this Scripture for the basis of his book *Kings and Priests*, points out that there are two callings: one for kings and another for priests. Some people are called to serve inside the church. They are the modern equivalent of the Old Testament priests who ministered in the Temple. But others are called to serve in the workplace, like the kings of the same period. Both calls are equally valid and interdependent.

Church Minister Calling

Priests or church ministers are called to the church domain of influence. They serve as pastors, ministry staff inside the church and in professional mission settings. In the New Testament, church ministers are referred to by using the terms pastor, teacher, evangelist, prophet, apostle, elder, deacon, priest, and missionary. God also uses church ministers in marketplace settings. For an example of this, refer to Corporate Chaplains of America (www.iamchap.org).

Workplace Minister Calling

Kings, or workplace ministers, are called to all of the other domains of influence: family, government, education, arts, communication, science, and business. Their purpose is to serve in the city. In many instances, God sometimes uses workplace ministers in a church ministry setting, e.g., the administrator of a church.

Kingly Men and Women

The kingly or workplace ministry calling includes both male and female. Genesis 1:27 reveals that *"God created man in his own image…male and female he created them."* They both reflect His character and nature. God has used men and women to accomplish His Kingdom plan as reflected throughout the Bible. In Galatians 3:28 God demonstrates that He is not a respecter of persons: *"There is neither…*

male nor female, for you are all one in Christ Jesus." God promises in these last days to use men and women to usher in His Kingdom. *"I will pour out my Spirit on all people. Your sons and daughters will prophesy, your old men will dream dreams, your young men will see visions. Even on my servants, both men and women, I will pour out my Spirit in those days"* (Joel 2:28-29).

God values unity. He has made men and women with different strengths to complement one another as reflections of Himself. *"Make every effort to keep the unity of the Spirit through the bond of peace. There is one body and one Spirit—just as you were called to one hope when you were called—one Lord, one faith, one baptism; one God and Father of all, who is over all and through all and in all"* (Ephesians 4:3-6).

"It was he who gave some to be apostles, some to be prophets, some to be evangelists, and some to be pastors and teachers, to prepare God's people for works of service, so that the body of Christ may be built up until we all reach unity in the faith and in the knowledge of the Son of God and become mature, attaining to the whole measure of the fullness of Christ" (Ephesians 4:11-13).

God expects both men and women to reach out to the lost. He will use available vessels to fulfill His plan.

Priesthood of All Believers

Every Christian is a minister. The New Testament replaced the Levitical priestly order with the "priesthood of all believers." 1 Peter 2:9 uses the word *"royal* (kingly) *priesthood"* to describe us. We recognize from this that ministry goes far beyond the scope of church-related activities. Ministry happens all over the city as Christians replicate the model presented in the book of Acts: *"They devoted themselves to the apostles' teaching and to the fellowship, to the breaking of bread and to prayer"* (Acts 2:42).

Terminology Used in Referring to Church and Workplace Ministers

The terms "church minister" and "workplace minister" bring clarity and unity. Instead of the terms "clergy" and "laity," which inappropriately segregate God's workers, it is preferable to refer to people called to the church domain as "church ministers" and those called to the marketplace domains as "workplace ministers."

There is no biblical basis for the misguided belief that the clergy are those called to professional full-time ministry while the laity—the rest of the people—are not. "Clergy" has its root in the Greek word *ekklesia*, which is the basis for the English word "ecclesiastic." It means the "ones called out." "Laity" has its roots in the word in the Greek word *laos*, which means "the people." Clergy and laity are popular terms for classifying church and workplace Christians, but they are not biblical ones. Instead of encouraging the role of workplace believers, they tend to diminish the role and imply that the laity are merely an audience.

The church is an assembly of God's people called out and called together for relationship with Him and with each other to accomplish His mission. "Church" comes from the Greek word ekklesia, which has two meanings. The first is "called together" or "called out." The second is an "assembly." This makes it an *assembly* of God's people *called out* and *called together* for relationship with Him and with each other to accomplish His mission.

Reflection and Discussion

1. Have you ever said or heard, "I'm just a layperson"? What was the context and how did it make you feel?

CHAPTER 5

WORKPLACE MINISTERS

> *I believe one of the next great moves of God is going to be*
> *through the believers in the workplace.*
> — *Dr. Billy Graham*

As the church becomes aware of the workplace movement, it poses some questions. Who are these workplace ministers? What percentage of people are called to workplace ministry? How do you identify a workplace minister? What is the strategic role of workplace ministers?

Definition of Workplace Ministers

Who are these workplace ministers and how do you actually define them? A definition of workplace ministers is crucial for identifying and understanding their operational role. There is no clear definition of a workplace minister found in current practitioner articles, books, or the Bible. By combining input from those sources, however, we propose this working definition of workplace ministers:

> ***Workplace Ministers*** *are leaders who are called and anointed by God to serve in their workplace with the purpose of transforming people and their environment for the Kingdom.*

This working definition includes a combination of thoughts based on the following authors and books:

- First-century Christians did not define "minister" as a clergy position but as service rendered by believers. It was a verb, not a noun.

- In his book *God@Work*, Rich Marshall defines workplace ministers as "…men and women whom God has placed in positions of leadership." This includes people in all areas of work life and covers a wide range of possibilities, from CEOs to minimum wage earners.

- In his book *Anointed for Business*, Ed Silvoso defines a person who is anointed for business in the context of bringing transformation to cities and nations through the marketplace.

Percentage of People Called to Minister in the Marketplace

God has called more people to minister in the marketplace than in religious settings. Dr. Bill Hamon, in his book *The Day of the Saints*, says that only five percent of the saints are called to be ministers behind a pulpit or on ministry staff, while ninety-five percent of saints are called by God to minister in the marketplace.

Men and women need to realize that not only is it okay to do ministry in the marketplace, but that God has deliberately *called* and *anointed* them for it. Since they spend so much time in the workplace, it is their primary area for introducing Kingdom principles.

Those called to the workplace already have the fullness of the Holy Spirit and His gifting to take the Kingdom of God there. They may use the same gifts and means as church ministers. Practically, this means doing business in the power of the Holy Spirit and having "church" all over the city as modeled in the second chapter of Acts.

Characteristics of Workplace Ministers

Workplace ministers could be described as people of honesty, integrity, moral excellence, high character, and influence. They are passionate about the Kingdom of God and usually have compassion for the hurting.

They think strategically and creatively about ways to impact their sphere of influence. They seek godly wisdom and are led by it as they discern opportunities and bring resources to influence their world in advancing the Kingdom. They intentionally utilize God's blessings for this purpose.

Workplace ministers are competent leaders with a strong desire to obey God's call by actively yielding to the Holy Spirit as they lead and teach others in areas of character, knowledge, skills, and spiritual maturity. They inspire, mentor and empower people who have potential. They respond to the Holy Spirit's leading in meeting the needs of people. In so doing, they are accomplishing both the Great Commandment and the Great Commission.

Four Levels of Involvement in the Workplace

Christians in the workplace demonstrate their convictions in various degrees of visibility. In his book *Anointed for Business*, Ed Silvoso identifies four levels of involvement in the workplace.

The first level of Christians in the workplace are those who are content merely to survive. Their aspiration is simply to remain believers while in the workplace. Some of them may even say that you cannot be a Christian and be a businessperson—that it is too tough a place.

The second level of Christians in the workplace are those who apply biblical principles to their work. This is where many Christians find themselves. They go to work, apply biblical principles to their activities, pray, read the Bible, witness, and keep a good testimony. They do not believe, however, that they can change their work environment.

The third level of Christians in the workplace are those who do their work in the power and fullness of the Holy Spirit. They do everything that the second-level Christians do, but they are also using the gifts of the Spirit and operating in His power. They recognize that the same gifts and power that operate inside the church building can operate inside the workplace.

The fourth level of Christians in the workplace are those who are involved in and committed to the transformation of their place of work. They do everything that the second- and third-level Christians do, but they do it with the full expectation that God will use them to transform their workplace—beginning with their niche. They are literally bringing the Kingdom of God into their place of work.

Testimony

Workplace Christians need to seek God for the best ways to use their influence and domains for the Kingdom. Here is a personal testimony from a workplace minister in the tourism industry. Let it help you see your work differently.

> *We, like many other businesspeople, have discovered the call of God on our business. For many years, my husband and I owned and operated three lodging establishments in Reno, Nevada. We thought about selling the business and "going into ministry" until someone challenged us to see our business* **as** *our ministry. Once we caught the vision, we proactively used our business to minister. We put Christian reading material in all the rooms, started a lending library, ministered to guests, held Bible studies with the employees, and provided rooms for abused women and the homeless. We also actively participated on local civic boards that made an impact on city affairs. We can personally testify that once we understood our calling, privileges, and responsibilities, we were able to actively steward our God-given resources for the harvest.*

Reflection and Discussion

1. What are your thoughts regarding the characteristics of workplace ministers?

2. What is the most you have hoped for in being a Christian influence in your workplace?

3. Look at the descriptions of the four levels of involvement in the workplace. In light of them, how would you assess your present level of involvement? What level do you aspire to reach?

4. What would it take to kick it up a notch? How can you move from where you are to the next level?

5. Can you share a testimony of a specific individual using their business or position of influence as a platform for ministry?

CHAPTER 6

THE CALLING

*God has specifically called and anointed workplace ministers to
transform their cities and nations, to bring in the harvest,
and to build the Kingdom of God.*

Have you been called to ministry? Are you sure? Many people,
whether still students or mid-life adults, experience painful confusion
over this question. Sometimes the answer is obscured by a simple
misunderstanding of the word "ministry."

Called to Fulltime Ministry in the Workplace

*Some Christians are called to fulltime ministry in the workplace
rather than in the church.* God does not view marketplace workers
as secular people and church workers as spiritual. God's call to be
a stay-at-home mom, a laborer, or president of a company is no less
holy than His call to be a pastor or a missionary. A position does not
define holiness; God's call defines it. A person's calling is based on
God's choosing. Obedience to God's call is the measure of a person's
success.

Each of us has a specific role for building up the body of Christ.
God has called marketplace Christians to various roles in the
workplace just as He has called church ministers to be preachers. He
has not called marketplace Christians to the pulpit of a church but to
a platform in their workplace. They do not exegete the Scriptures, but
they live them. They are frontline troops whose platform may be a
babysitting co-op, an executive's desk, or a contractor's pickup. It may

be a politician's influence or a salesperson's briefcase. Their work is their platform to develop relationships 40+ hours per week. Their "congregation" at work consists of the people they touch: fellow workers and their families, customers, clients, associates, and suppliers.

We can turn an ordinary job into an extraordinary mission if we realize that God has specifically called us to our place of work as an opportunity to influence others for His Kingdom. Some call this the 9 to 5 window.

The workplace is the greatest mission field of our day. We have outstanding opportunities to build relationships with co-workers. God has uniquely equipped workplace leaders to touch people within their own circles of influence—people who are unreached by traditional Christian services. The Bible says, *"Whatever you do, work at it with all your heart, as working for the Lord, not for men"* (Colossians 3:23).

Misinterpreting the Call

A partially understood call may lead believers to enter into a church ministry rather than a workplace ministry domain. When workplace Christians have a passion and zeal for spiritual things, they (and their pastors) may interpret it as a call to fulltime church ministry. Workplace Christians need to realize that receiving a call to ministry does not necessarily mean leaving their current workplace position. In many cases, it is not a call to leave their current position as much as it is to discover God's call into that very arena—the place where God wants to anoint and bless their service. When people misinterpret their marketplace calling as a church calling, they may choose a second-best role and be less effective for the Kingdom.

Workplace Position as a Platform for Ministry

Workplace Christians need to recognize their call to the workplace.

Our position in the workplace is the vehicle God has given us to bring the Kingdom of God into unique places to touch people. When workplace Christians understand that the Lord may be calling them to make their role at work their platform for ministry, there is a release of freedom and power for them to fulfill their call. Once they understand this, they are ready to steward their God-given resources.

Workplace Christians need to know that a call to their area of work is equivalent to their pastor's call to the local church. Pastors should help workplace Christians recognize their marketplace calling and validate it. They can play a vital role in helping business owners recognize that their businesses are extremely effective platforms for ministry.

You Have Been Given a Calling by God

You do not choose your calling; your calling chooses you. God designed you with a plan in mind. Your personality, skills, talents, interests and longings are unique to you. They are God-given tools for fulfilling your purpose—serving others and honoring Him. Using the tools He has given you in the way He has planned feels like doing something you were meant to do. It is uncovering and following your personal destiny; you feel the pleasure of contributing something worthwhile to the public good, something that would not exist without you, something you are good at and something you enjoy. Your calling will include a passion for what you do. Reflect on your calling by reading Psalm 90.

Identify Your Calling

It is of the utmost importance to identify your calling. Whatever your purpose and calling are, they will always involve serving people. Consider these four characteristics of a calling:

1. *It is unique to each individual.* Each person reflects only a small but beautiful part of the whole. Together, we are involved

in bringing the Creator's work to fulfillment.

2. *It requires certain preconditions.* It requires talent. It must fit our abilities. It involves loving the long hours, frustrations, small steps forward, and struggles that accompany its activity.

3. *It brings a sense of enjoyment and renewed energy.* True calling reveals its presence by the enjoyment and sense of renewed energy its practice yields.

4. *It is often difficult to discover.* Much patient searching may be required before we recognize what will later seem obvious.

Remain in Your Calling

Twice Paul urges us to remain in the vocation to which God has called us. In 1 Corinthians 7:17 he says, *"Each one should retain the place in life that the Lord assigned to him and to which God has called him."* And verse 20 says, *"Each one should remain in the situation which he was in when God called him."*

To have influence in our work and be effective, it is important to remain in our calling. This is counter-cultural to the American lifestyle. The average American's working life includes three different vocations and fifteen different jobs.

Reflection and Discussion

1. Do you really believe that your work is your calling from God? Do you really believe that you are fulfilling God's calling?

2. Do you really believe that your work is every bit as holy in God's eyes as that of your pastor or any other leader in the local church?

3. Do you see yourself and your work Monday through Friday as being just as important to God as what goes on in your church on Sunday?

4. What does the word "ministry" in your workplace mean to you?

5. Can you identify your work as your platform for ministry?

6. Have you wrestled with the thought of "leaving everything and going into the ministry"? Why?

7. Have you, as a workplace Christian, ever felt like a second-class citizen in the Kingdom?

8. Discard the deception that you are not a minister. Let the truth of God's Word wash away all unbiblical distortions regarding your identity and calling. Agree with God that you are a minister called to the marketplace.

CHAPTER 7

THE ANOINTING

The anointing which you have received from Him remains in you.
—1 John 2:27

Most of us have read verses about anointing the sick with oil as we pray for their healing. And we recall the practice of prophets and priests to anoint the kings of Israel and Judah at their installation. Beyond that, however, our exposure gets thin, leaving us with a fuzzy, mystical concept that seems to have little meaning in twenty-first century life. This chapter demonstrates the importance of anointing and how it relates to you.

Definition of Anointed

"Anointed" applies to a person chosen and empowered by the Holy Spirit for a divinely sanctioned assignment. As defined by the *Enhanced Strong's Lexicon,* "anointing" means "enduing Christians with the gifts of the Holy Spirit." The anointing is God's Spirit overflowing into a human life consecrated to God.

God is the one who anoints. "God…anointed us, set his seal of ownership on us, and put his Spirit in our hearts" (2 Corinthians 1:21-22). God looks at a person's heart. God is the one who releases people into their anointed ministry. His anointing is powerfully available to marketplace Christians.

To be anointed means fulltime consecration to God and His work. Part-time anointing, or anointing for part-time ministry is not found in the Bible. In the Old Testament, oil was used in the anointing of a person, an item, or a place that had been set aside for divine use. *"Take the anointing oil and anoint the tabernacle and everything in it; consecrate it and all its furnishings, and it will be holy"* (Exodus 40:9).

When a person was anointed, a large amount of oil, which is symbolic of the Holy Spirit, was poured on the head to symbolize that the totality of the person was set aside. This was God's command to Moses for consecrating the priests: *"Take the anointing oil and anoint him by pouring it on his head"* (Exodus 29:7).

The anointing was always for fulltime consecration. Kings, priests, prophets and places were set aside in toto for divine service. Abundant, overflowing, enveloping, transforming anointing is what we see in Psalm 133:1-3; *"How good and pleasant it is when brothers live together in unity! It is like precious oil poured on the head, running down on the beard, running down on Aaron's beard, down upon the collar of his robes. It is as if the dew of Hermon were falling on Mount Zion. For there the LORD bestows his blessing, even life forevermore."*

Definition of Anointed for the Workplace

*To be anointed for the workplace means to be set aside by God for service in the marketplace t*o use your job as a ministry vehicle to bring transformation to the marketplace, so that the gospel will reach everyone in your sphere of influence (adapted from Silvoso, p. 33). Notice the four specific points in this definition:

1. To be set aside by God for service in the marketplace
2. To use your job as a ministry vehicle
3. To bring transformation to the marketplace
4. So that the gospel will reach everyone in your sphere of influence

Purpose of Anointed Workplace Ministers

The anointing is to transform people and their environment. It is for the ministry of serving others—not just being a witness, but bringing transformation. When Paul told King Agrippa the words Jesus had spoken to him, he stated this ministry purpose well. *"...I am sending you to them to open their eyes and turn them from darkness to light, and from the power of Satan to God, so that they may receive forgiveness of sins and a place among those who are sanctified by faith in me"* (Acts 26:17-18).

We believe that the Lord is sending an anointing for powerful ministry in the marketplace arena. He is anointing workplace leaders to be ministers in the marketplace—to pray with power, to witness, to bring signs and wonders, to receive godly insight, to create wealth by means of the empowerment of the Holy Spirit, to think strategically about transforming their workplace, their city, and their nation.

Operating in the Anointing

Operating in the anointing is allowing God to do His work so that the will of God will be done on earth. If God has given you an anointing, be careful and watch over it. You must nurture it, use it, and be responsible with it. Anointing demands consecration and serious, disciplined preparation. Your level of anointing depends on your level of holiness in dying to self every day, being available to do God's will and accepting the results.

God will expand your sphere of influence until you reach the level He has chosen for you. Anointed workplace Christians must decide to obey God and use His anointing. *"You were faithful with a few things, I will put you in charge of many things..."* (Matthew 25:21). The Lord moves His servants from "a few things" to "many things" simply because of their faithfulness.

Consider these Old Testament examples of supernatural anointing. Although there is no record of these men participating in a ceremonial anointing, it is clear that God anointed them for special service according to His plan. Noah received a special anointing to build the ark. Joseph received anointing to run the Egyptian empire. Moses obtained anointing to lead the people of Israel thru the wilderness. Joshua received anointing to take Jericho and the Promised Land. Daniel received anointing to be the prime minister of Babylon. Nehemiah received anointing to repair the wall.

Fallacies that Undermine Anointed Workplace Ministers

Several fallacies undermine God's calling on those anointed for workplace ministry:

Fallacy #1: *There is a God-ordained division between clergy and laity.* The truth is that there are no first- or second-class people in God's Kingdom.

Fallacy #2: *The church is to operate primarily inside a building.* It is fine that we have buildings, but the church is not limited to them. We pray for the day when we will devote ourselves continually to the work of God in the workplace, witnessing manifestations of His presence all over the city. God is birthing something new. Church buildings will no longer be adequate. As in the book of Acts, we may have to go into stadiums and arenas in order to hold the crowds.

Fallacy #3: *People involved in business, education, and government cannot be as spiritual as those serving in traditional church ministry can.* We have wrongly dichotomized the secular and spiritual worlds. We are not to believe the lie that workplace Christians are not as spiritual as those who have gone to Bible school or seminary.

Fallacy #4: *The primary role of people in the workplace is to make money to support the vision of those "in the ministry."* Even though marketplace Christians are called to do this, it is not the totality of their call.

Reflection and Discussion

1. Do you believe your God-given power is to be exercised primarily within the church or in the workplace?

2. Explain how any of the four fallacies have undermined God's anointing on your life for workplace ministry.

3. Name five people in your sphere of influence or personal network who may be called and anointed to fulltime ministry in the workplace. (Keep in mind that fulltime does not necessarily mean professional or paid.)

4. Pray in agreement with another person: I am anointed for my place of work. My job is my platform. My workplace is my congregation. I have been called by God to bring His Kingdom to my place of work.

CHAPTER 8

THE MARKETPLACE

Indeed, as with first-century Christianity, it all begins in the marketplace,
where the disciples of Jesus daily rub shoulders with the lost.
—Bill McCartney, Promise Keepers

Throughout the Bible, the marketplace was the center of activity, the place where God called ordinary men and women to do great and mighty works. We see it in the Old Testament, during the lifetime of Jesus, and during the growth of the early church. It is no different today; the marketplace is still the center of activity, and God is still calling ordinary people to do great works there.

Marketplace in the World

The marketplace is the focus of action in every community throughout the world. Everything revolves around it.

The marketplace is a combination of, business, education, government and the church. It is the heart and circulation of the city, and through its combined arteries, the life of a city flows.

Marketplace in the Bible

Examine the Scriptures from a marketplace perspective. When reading the Bible, we tend to focus on who God is, what Jesus did, who we are, and how we relate to God. That's good, but try reading and examining the Scriptures through your marketplace glasses. You will get a new and richer perspective on how to apply the truth on

Monday as you relate to others and to all of the tangibles at work. Allow the truth of the Scriptures to set you free in the marketplace.

As seen in the Scriptures, most Old Testament leaders were deeply involved in everyday marketplace issues. Abraham was a successful and wealthy businessman in the Near East (Genesis chapters 12-25). Joseph ran an Egyptian empire (Genesis chapters 41-50). Job was the wealthiest man in the country of Uz (Job 1:3).

David started in the shepherding business and later became the King of Israel. He did not accept a sacred-secular dichotomy, believing that fighting Goliath was a spiritual enterprise but running his business was a secular one. God was central in both. Imagine young David as a shepherd trying to deal with lions and bears without God's protection and empowering.

Fortunately, he understood the source of his help very clearly. Listen as he tries to convince King Saul to let him do battle with Goliath. *"Your servant has been keeping his father's sheep. When a lion or a bear came and carried off a sheep from the flock, I went after it, struck it and rescued the sheep from its mouth. When it turned on me, I seized it by its hair, struck it and killed it. Your servant has killed both the lion and the bear; this uncircumcised Philistine will be like one of them, because he has defied the armies of the living God. The LORD who delivered me from the paw of the lion and the paw of the bear will deliver me from the hand of this Philistine"* (1 Samuel 17: 34-37).

Jesus and the Marketplace

The world's creator was born in the marketplace. The second chapter of Luke tells us that the stable of an inn hosted the birth of Jesus. His first visitors were shepherds; some were probably employees, and others, small-business owners.

Jesus spent many years as a carpenter in business. He was more recognizable as a businessman than as a rabbi or a ruler. Mark 6:3 says, *"Isn't this the carpenter? Isn't this Mary's son...?"* People in his hometown described Him as "the carpenter's son" (Matthew 13:55).

Many people engaged Jesus' professional services and purchased products made by His hands. They ate at tables He made, walked through doors He made, lived under roofs supported by beams that He cut and fit. Some of them may have driven oxen that sported harnesses He made.

Jesus was a well-established artisan, a craftsman. He had to learn His trade, receiving training as a carpenter between the ages of seven and twelve. By the time of His baptism, He had been in business as a craftsman for over 20 years. This means that Jesus spent more than fifty percent of His life as a carpenter before beginning a preaching ministry in the workplace.

We can assume that Jesus' shop was profitable, that it was large enough and made enough money to support a family of eight or more. *"Isn't his mother's name Mary, and aren't his brothers James, Joseph, Simon and Judas? Aren't all his sisters with us?"* (Matthew 13:55-56).

We can also assume that as a rabbi, He had to master a trade and exercise it honestly to support Himself so that He could teach without payment. As any entrepreneur, Jesus would have to deal with business issues such as cost of goods and labor, supply and demand, competitive pricing, return on investment, taxes, maintenance, and replacement of equipment. He was tempted in every way that any modern businessman is.

Of Jesus' 132 public appearances in the New Testament, 122 were in the marketplace. Jesus mingled with all sorts of people all over the city. He was a real person and an informed leader who confronted real problems.

Of the 52 parables Jesus told, 45 had a workplace context. The following parables show that He was familiar with the marketplace and its operations:

- Construction (Matthew 7:24-27)
- Wine making (Luke 5:37-38)
- Farming (Mark 4:2-20)

- Buried treasure and ownership rights (Matthew 13:44)
- Ranching (Matthew 18:12-13)
- Management and labor (Matthew 20:1-16)
- Family-owned businesses (Matthew 21:28-31)
- Hostile takeovers (Luke 20:9-19)
- Return on investment (Matthew 25:14-30)
- Harvest timing (Mark 13:27-32)
- Management criteria (Luke 12:35-48)
- Determining priorities and acceptable levels of sacrifice (Luke 14:25-33)
- Need to expose corruption (Mark 11:15-17)

Jesus performed business miracles in the marketplace. A miracle is a divine intervention into human affairs. He produced a tremendous return on a young boy's investment, turning five loaves and two fish into a banquet to feed *"5,000 men, besides women and children"* (Matthew 14:13-21). Later, he performed a similar miracle, feeding *"4,000 besides women and children"* (Matthew 15:29-38). He transformed water into wine at a wedding (John 2:1-10). He enabled the disciples to catch an enormous quantity of fish, producing what must have been their most profitable day ever (Luke 5:1-9 and John 21:1-6). Jesus also enabled Peter to catch a fish with a coin in its mouth to pay taxes (Matthew 17:24-27).

Jesus' financial needs were provided. The Magi visited Jesus when He was a baby, presenting him with expensive gifts (Matthew 2:10-11). He was a guest of honor in the homes of wealthy people (Luke 11:37;14:7; 19:5). Joseph of Arimathea provided a deluxe burial place for Him (Matthew 27:57-60). A group of wealthy women contributed to the support of Jesus and the twelve disciples (Luke 8:1-3). He always had adequate resources for His ministry and for the support of those traveling with Him.

The Disciples and the Marketplace

The disciples all came from the marketplace. Jesus called twelve workplace individuals rather then those in the clergy to build His church. Not one of the twelve was a leader in the temple or the synagogue.

Jesus recruited His disciples in the marketplace, not in the temple. Peter and Andrew were professional fisherman caught in the middle of action (Matthew 4:18-19). John and James were also professional fisherman, repairing their nets when Jesus called them (Matthew 4:21-22). Matthew was a tax collector in his office when Jesus saw him (Matthew 9:9).

The Gospels were written by marketplace leaders. Matthew was a retired tax collector, similar to an IRS agent. Mark was a scion of a wealthy family, the equivalent of a private foundation's CEO. Mark's mother, Mary, was the one in whose house many met to pray for Peter's release from prison (Acts 12:12-17). Luke was a medical doctor. John was a fisherman.

The Early Church and the Marketplace

The church was conceived in a private home, a non-religious setting (Acts 1:13, 15). Rather than beginning in a temple or synagogue, the church was conceived in the upper room of a private home. We know it was a large house because the twelve were *staying* there. Since they were joined there by 120 believers, the house was most likely owned by a wealthy person.

The disciples held church all over the city every day, several times a day. Although the church was conceived in the upper room, it was not born until the disciples went out into the marketplace where the Word of God was preached and 3,000 believed in Christ. When the Holy Spirit had fallen on the disciples in the upper room, the first thing He did was to *get them out* rather than *keep them in*. In turn, these 3,000 converts held church all over the city.

Most of their activity took place in homes, an extension of the marketplace. The believers went to the temple for prayer (Acts 2:26; 3:1) but most of their activities were in homes. They met "house to house" where they lived and worked (Acts 2:44-47 NASB).

Early Christians made the marketplace the focal point of their ministry. They saw the marketplace as their parish, their business as a platform. To them, witnessing to unbelievers was a lifestyle. The early church was comfortable in non-religious settings as they naturally presented the gospel to the people they encountered.

As the apostles performed signs and wonders in the marketplace, Jerusalem experienced transformation. The high priest accused the apostles with these words, *"...you have filled Jerusalem with your teaching..."* (Acts 5:28). After the initial 3000 converts on the day of Pentecost, growth continued to be explosive. *"So the word of God spread. The number of disciples in Jerusalem increased rapidly, and a large number of priests became obedient to the faith"* (Acts 6:7).

- The needs of the poor and the widows were met (Acts 6:1-7).
- The hungry were fed, and sick were healed (Acts 2:45; 3:2-8).
- Solomon's Colonnade became a place for signs and wonders (Acts 5:12-14).
- The streets and sidewalks were turned into evangelistic venues for healing the sick (Acts 5:15).
- Multitudes from nearby cities flooded Jerusalem (Acts 5:16).
- Even the Sanhedrin, the highest Jewish tribunal during the Greek and Roman periods, was positively influenced by the gospel (Acts 5:33-39).

Marketplace Leaders in the Early Church

Marketplace leaders played a vital role in the emergence, establishment, and expansion of the early church.

They were excellent leaders who were equipped rapidly for ministry. None of the leaders in the early church were priests or leaders in the temple; they were business people and government officials. Already leaders in the city, they came to Christ through a power encounter and took positions of leadership in the church. They experienced God's dramatic transformation and were passionate about their newfound faith, ministering to the lost on a daily basis.

They were capable of both ministry and business. The marketplace leaders in the early church blended their work and ministry activities.

- Paul, Aquila, and Priscilla made and sold tents (Acts 18:1-3). Paul's business in Ephesus was profitable enough to provide for him, his team and needy people (Acts 20:33-35).

- Lydia, the first European convert, was a wealthy wholesaler of purple cloth, an expensive fabric used in the garments of nobles and kings. Shortly after her conversion, the marketplace experienced a power encounter involving a slave girl with a spirit of divination (Acts 16:14-21).

- Dorcas, a designer and manufacturer of delicate inner garments, was successful enough to be *"always doing good and helping the poor"* (Acts 9:36).

- The Ethiopian eunuch was the finance minister in charge of all the treasury of Candace, queen of Ethiopia (Acts 8:27).

- Erastus was the city director of public works (Romans 16:23).

- Theophilus (Luke 1:3 and Acts 1:1) is thought to have been a high-ranking government official.

- Philemon (Philemon 1) is thought to have been a wealthy, generous leader.

- Peter, a fisherman, was a guest in the home of Simon, a tanner, when Cornelius, a senior military officer sent for him.

These leaders were capable of understanding theological truths. A most difficult theological truth to grasp in a Jewish context—that Gentiles can be saved without becoming Jews first—was entrusted to them (Acts 10:1-48).

Growth of the Early Church

The Church grew as recognized leaders were selected to partner with the apostles. Workplace Christians were selected to fix a deficiency in the food distribution system that threatened the growth and harmony of the church (Acts 6:1-6). *"So the word of God spread. The number of disciples in Jerusalem increased rapidly, and a large number of priests became obedient to the faith"* (Acts 6:7).

The Word of God quickly spread in Jerusalem, with many priests even becoming obedient to the faith. Stephen performed great signs and wonders, raising the opposition of those unable to refute his wisdom. When he died at their hands, Phillip picked up the task of performing miracles in Samaria, outside of Jerusalem. An angel sent Phillip on a specific mission in which he was able to lead another key business leader to the Lord—the eunuch in charge of all the treasury of Ethiopia.

Thirty-nine of the 40 divine interventions recorded in the book of Acts occurred in the marketplace. Of the 40 extraordinary manifestations of God's power, only one happened in a religious venue: the healing of the lame man at the temple gate called Beautiful (Acts 3:1-10).

Persecution forced the church to move out of Jerusalem. During the siege of Jerusalem in 69 A.D., many members of the church were forced to flee the city. After the destruction of the temple, Jerusalem was no longer viewed as the center of Christianity. Instead, the church's international headquarters moved from Jerusalem, a religious city, to Antioch, a merchant city located on important trading routes. Some scholars believe that God may have been behind the destruction of the temple in order to move the Christians out as Jesus had commanded in the Great Commission. Their religious fortress had prevented them from the effectiveness He desired.

When Paul, Aquila and Priscilla focused on taking the gospel into the marketplace of Corinth, people were saved, power encounters happened, and the church grew rapidly. The following diagram shows how Paul, a church minister, partnered with Aquila and Priscilla, workplace ministers. Paul went into business, and Aquila and Priscilla went into church work. Together they set up a tent-making operation in the marketplace (Acts 18:1-3).

Paul	Partners with…	Aquila & Priscilla
Church Minister		Workplace Ministers
went into business		went into ministry

At first Paul attempted to reach people through the synagogue, but the Jews opposed and abused him. Realizing that the city had many people who needed to be saved, he declared, *"From now on I will go to the Gentiles"* (Acts 18:6). In a vision, God told Paul, *"Do not be afraid; keep on speaking, do not be silent. For I am with you…"* (Acts 18:9-10). God divinely reassured him of his call to the city.

Through all of this, God was at work behind the scenes, moving the church to the marketplace. Paul moved his base of operation out of the synagogue to a nearby house, most likely the one that housed his tent-making business. There, Paul was able to teach daily rather than just on the Sabbath. In his marketplace ministry setting, *"many of the Corinthians who heard him believed and were baptized"* (Acts 18:8). Greek Gentiles were Paul's most receptive audience.

Ephesus experienced radical transformation. Paul preached in the marketplace daily for two years, and God did extraordinary miracles through him. Ephesus, a demon-driven economy and citadel of evil, experienced radical transformation as its marketplace witnessed dramatic power encounters (Acts 19:8-20).

Encounters happened "in practically the whole province of Asia" (Acts 19:26). If Paul had confined himself to the synagogue, he never could have reached all of Asia—but neither could he have reached it without the synagogue.

Twenty-first century churches may be equivalent to the first century synagogue. We will not see transformation in a city by having church once a week. A weekly church gathering is to equip the saints with biblical doctrine for the work of the ministry. If equipped workplace leaders would bring the Kingdom of God to the marketplace on a daily basis, we could see a repeat of what happened in Corinth and Ephesus.

Ministry and Work Blended

First century Christians did not see working in the marketplace and serving in the church as mutually exclusive activities. They did not necessarily leave their jobs to do fulltime ministry. *"You yourselves know that these hands of mine have supplied my own needs and the needs of my companions"* (Acts 20:34). Even Jesus' followers may have remained in their work while simultaneously conducting fulltime ministry.

Paul, Aquila, and Priscilla simultaneously conducted business and ministry. Paul clearly stated to the Corinthians, *"the Lord has commanded that those who preach the gospel should receive their living from the gospel"* (1 Corinthians 9:14). But then he quickly added, *"But I have not used any of these rights. And I am not writing this in the hope that you will do such things for me. I would rather die than have anyone deprive me of this boast…that in preaching the gospel I may offer it free of charge, and so not make use of my rights in preaching it"* (1 Corinthians 9:15-18).

To the Thessalonians he said, *"We were not idle when we were with you, nor did we eat anyone's food without paying for it. On the contrary, we worked night and day, laboring and toiling so that we would not be a burden to any of you"* (2 Thessalonians 3:8).

What a privilege it is to be in a position to minister like Paul, yielding the right to be paid for it because God had given him the ability to support himself!

Reflection and Discussion

1. Prior to reading this chapter, what was your view of Jesus and His relationship to the marketplace? How has it changed?

2. Have you thought of Jesus as a marketplace person or manager? Explain.

3. Why do you believe Jesus intentionally chose marketplace people who were not members of the religious establishment?

4. What new perspective did you receive on the marketplace and the early church?

5. Have you thought that working in the marketplace and serving in the church were mutually exclusive activities? Explain.

6. How has the arbitrary classification of "fulltime" and "part-time" ministry affected the church?

7. Reflect on God saying to you, "You want to get people saved in the church, and I have lost people in the city." Reflect on the idea that the place you call work is a place God calls ministry. The gift of the Holy Spirit and the anointing of God are already in you to bring the Kingdom of God into your workplace.

8. Reflect on the thought that being in a secular job does not disqualify you from fulltime ministry. Do you believe that you cannot understand doctrine and teach the Bible because you haven't gone to Bible school? Do you believe that your teacher is the Holy Spirit, your source is the Word of God, and the Word is able to equip you for every good work?

CHAPTER 9

TRANSFORMING CITIES AND NATIONS

Societal transformation is high on God's agenda and the chief catalytic force to bring it about will be Christians ministering in the marketplace.
—Peter Wagner, Wagner Leadership Institute

...men of Issachar, who understood the times and knew what Israel should do.—1 Chronicles 12:32

The workplace ministry movement may be more appropriately called "workplace transformation." Workplace ministers play important roles in transforming their workplaces as they bring in the harvest, execute justice, and revolutionize systems. Their light must penetrate the darkness of the workplace.

Bring in Provision for the Harvest

It has been said that "Priests bring the vision; kings bring the provision." Providing resources and bringing in necessary funds to accomplish the vision is one of the purposes for Christians working in the marketplace.

Workplace ministers have the gifts and abilities to generate wealth for the Kingdom. They do this by giving from their own wealth and by providing creative strategies for its use and multiplication. The following Scriptures say that the wealth of the wicked is laid up for the righteous. *"To the man who pleases him, God gives wisdom, knowledge and happiness, but to the sinner he gives the task of gathering and storing up wealth to hand it over to the one who pleases*

God" (Ecclesiastes 2:26). *"...a sinner's wealth is stored up for the righteous"* (Proverbs 13:22).

Since this is God's plan, He will anoint people to go after those resources. Workplace Christians need to pray and seek the Lord for His strategies so the wealth of the wicked can be transferred to the righteous, creating resources for Kingdom work.

Execute Judgment, Justice, and Righteousness

Although bringing in provision for the end-time harvest is *one* major role of workplace Christians, the *major* role is to bring about transformation.

God instructs His kings to execute judgment, justice, and righteousness. The prophet Jeremiah clearly reveals God's heart for His people and the responsibility He places on their leaders. *"Hear the word of the LORD, O king of Judah, you who sit on David's throne—you, your officials and your people who come through these gates. This is what the LORD says: Do what is just and right. Rescue from the hand of his oppressor the one who has been robbed. Do no wrong or violence to the alien, the fatherless or the widow, and do not shed innocent blood in this place. For if you are careful to carry out these commands, then kings who sit on David's throne will come through the gates of this palace, riding in chariots and on horses, accompanied by their officials and their people. But if you do not obey these commands, declares the LORD, I swear by myself that this palace will become a ruin"* (Jeremiah 22:2-5).

When the queen of Sheba visited Solomon, she perceived God's favor and rightly deduced, *"...Because of the love of your God for Israel and his desire to uphold them forever, he has made you king over them, to maintain justice and righteousness"* (2 Chronicles 9:8).

Workplace leaders can be influential in bringing justice and righteousness to the poverty stricken and those oppressed by racial or gender discrimination in the workplace. Funding mercy ministries is a good thing, but it is not enough. Workplace leaders need to be proactive in both redeeming people and lifting them out of their present state.

God gives workplace leaders the power to lift oppression, to care for social outcasts and the needy. Through marketplace reconciliation, leaders embrace the oppressed and disenfranchised people of our cities, tangibly meeting their needs.

Workplace ministers initiate making Jesus real in a broken world. Only as we recognize that each of us is called to minister, and we say yes to that call, can the church fulfill its mission to be the hands of Christ in a hurting world. This is illustrated by a story called Christ's Hands in a Broken World.

> *One of the casualties of World War II was a statue of Christ that had stood in the center of a French village. Villagers carefully saved the shattered pieces, waiting until the war was over to rebuild the statue. It became apparent during the process that Christ's hands were missing. The villagers didn't know what to do. Should they leave the incomplete statue standing or should they take it down? Only after someone placed a small hand-painted sign at the statue's base were the villagers able to agree that the statue should remain as it was. The sign read, "Christ has no hands but ours."*

Revolutionize Systems

The marketplace is comprised of sin-darkened cities sick with greed and lust. We believe that most demonic forces focus on the command centers that control our cities and economic system—the businesses, educational and governmental institutions that remain unredeemed. These structures are now controlled by Satan.

God, however, wants to change structures controlled by Satan. God has strategically placed Christians in the workplace as soldiers closest to Satan's command and control centers. When workplace Christians are properly equipped and empowered, they bring light that offers a sharp contrast to these corrupt structures.

As Christ's ambassadors, we have the power and authority to redeem business, educational, and governmental structures. God has given us the power not only to make a difference but also to alter these structures. *"And these signs will accompany those who believe: In my name they will drive out demons; they will speak in new tongues; they will pick up snakes with their hands [expose lurking threats]; and when they drink deadly poison [evil schemes], it will not hurt them at all; they will place their hands on sick people, and they will get well"* (Mark 16:17-18).

With God's divine power, we may do greater works than even Jesus did. *"I tell you the truth, anyone who has faith in me will do what I have been doing. He will do even greater things than these, because I am going to the Father. And I will do whatever you ask in my name, so that the Son may bring glory to the Father. You may ask me for anything in my name, and I will do it"* (John 14:12-15).

However, many Christians feel like spiritual POWs in the workplace. They believe that the best they can do at their place of work is to be a good witness, operate their organization based on biblical principles, and maybe lead someone to Christ. They have not comprehended the possibility of seeing their workplace transformed—pushing back the satanic infrastructure and using prayer to usher in the Kingdom.

When marketplace Christians realize that they have a divine call, along with the anointing and the authority to exercise God's power in the workplace, God's Kingdom will begin to replace Satan's strongholds. The marketplace will become a place of dynamic ministry and spiritual transformation, revolutionizing cities and nations.

Bring Societal Transformation to the Workplace

God designed the church to be countercultural, producing transformation rather than being a mere subculture satisfied with survival in isolation. Jesus commanded His disciples to take the Kingdom of God to the people. He compared His Kingdom to leaven, light, salt and seeds that would infiltrate, shine, preserve, or sprout in the physical world. The church was not to be a fixed, physical monument but a living movement that freely expanded. The church was not to assimilate itself into society but to transform society.

The church transforms society through the workplace. Christians are already strategically positioned in the marketplace—a place filled with people who don't know Jesus. Every workplace Christian has an area of influence—a God-given platform from which to reclaim, redeem and restore those lost to the Kingdom.

Societal transformation occurs when God's Kingdom is brought into the workplace. Bringing Kingdom principles into the workplace fosters unity, harmony, mercy, respect, and caring for others. It brings order and peace out of chaos. It promotes unity in diversity, even as the Trinity is both diverse and united. It produces structural and social transformation by changing the environmental system. God's Kingdom can penetrate all areas of influence as anointed workplace leaders rely on God's wisdom to bring it to their workplace.

Transformation occurs in the marketplace because of God-given authority. Our authority as marketplace ministers is known in the heavenly places. Demonic forces know that faith-filled Christians have authority to bring down the kingdom of darkness in the marketplace.

Acts 19:11-16 provides a fascinating example of the power of a believer known in heavenly places versus a counterfeit who is not. *"God did extraordinary miracles through Paul, so that even handkerchiefs and aprons that had touched him were taken to the sick, and their illnesses were cured and the evil spirits left them. Some Jews who went around driving out evil spirits tried to invoke the name of the Lord Jesus over those who were demon-possessed. They would say, 'In the name of Jesus, whom Paul preaches, I command you to come out.' Seven sons of Sceva, a Jewish chief priest, were doing this. (One day) the evil spirit answered them, 'Jesus I know, and I know about Paul, but who are you?' Then the man who had the evil spirit jumped on them and overpowered them all. He gave them such a beating that they ran out of the house naked and bleeding."*

Any authority that resides in our humanity is destined to produce temporary results at best. Transformation requires the use of authentic, God-given authority.

The Kingdom of God transforms not just individuals but also the environment. We, as workplace Christians, have authority over the demonic forces that impoverish the nation.

Consider the Hollywood executives who have justified their constant barrage of sex-and debauchery-soaked movies by saying, "We're only releasing what the public wants to see!" Many of them refused to recognize a viable audience for stories and characters that extol biblical virtues. *The Passion of the Christ* clearly demonstrated such an audience.

Or consider the city of Almalonga, Guatemala, known for crime, drunkenness and family abuse. Small groups of people prayed for the city and the land. The Gospel transformed the community. The land was healed, yielding a 1000 percent increase in produce. Now known for their fine produce and fertile fields, they are even leasing land outside of the city.

Let Your Light Shine in the Workplace

Our light shines when we act in contrast to the ways of the world. Jesus said, *"Let your light shine before men, that they may see your good deeds and praise your Father in Heaven"* (Matthew 5:16).

Light shines the brightest when the contrast is the greatest. It is good when we do works of righteousness among the saints, but they do not stand out as powerfully as they do against the backdrop of the marketplace. When we act in ways that are consistent with Christ's teachings and in contrast to the world, our light shines. It shines when we:

- Respond in kindness to our competitors.
- Give employees another chance.
- Keep our word in spite of the fact that it costs us to do so.

- Honor all men in positions both above and below us.
- Don't demand the privilege that our position affords us in the eyes of the world.
- Don't take advantage of others for ourselves.
- Use our money to build people, rather than using our people to make money.

Community Transformation

Workplace transformation is a catalyst for community transformation. A community is transformed by the power of God and is characterized by every facet of life submitting to God's authority. It is not measured by a standard of perfection but rather by the degree of its improvement. Some signs of a transformed community are a new sense of community purpose and identity, changed ecology, church growth, the flowing of supernatural power, a decrease in divorce, crime, and suicide rates.

Community transformation begins as committed people earnestly seek the Lord's presence and His heart for the city, praying and fasting for the power of God's Spirit to come into their community. As they focus on the community, they apply their faith that God is able to move mountains.

Core Principles

Consider these core principles for community transformation.

God wants to be invited into our communities. God wants us to invite His transformation. We invite Him by praying and fasting, by the cry of our heart to seek His presence in our city. In order for us to be change agents in the city, we must first be changed. A heart of holy humility draws God's presence, and with it, a new sense of identity. Isaiah, speaking to God's people in Zion says, *"The nations will see your righteousness, and all kings your glory; you will be called by a new name that the mouth of the Lord will bestow"* (Isaiah 62:2). This has always been God's desire—His followers faithfully demonstrating His character so distinctly that it is obvious, earning them a new identity and even a new name.

Large-scale revival begins with individual obedience. Revival doesn't usually fall from the sky on masses of people. It begins when a person or two or three respond to their own sins with heartfelt anguish. Most often there is public confession, repentance, seeking of forgiveness (both from God and the people involved), and making restitution. As others witness this transparency, God often brings conviction to their hearts. A chain reaction begins, and no one knows where or when it ends.

God requires biblical unity. Unity comes as a byproduct of relationships. When two or three gather in prayer with holy, humble hearts, God's presence is there, and with it comes unity.

Breakthrough prayer releases revival. God honors fervent, persistent prayer that rises from submissive, repentant, desperate hearts. Being in touch with God's heart for the city enables workplace ministers to pray with knowledge for its destiny—praying with a results orientation because of what God has shown them.

God's work will always be unique. God wants to be invited, but He comes on His own terms. The wind of the Spirit, impossible to predict, moves at God's bidding and in His timing. God is too creative to delight in repeat performances, often choosing to enter a community through the backdoor.

God uses servant leaders. God wants committed leaders who will direct people into the Kingdom—leaders who count the cost, stay the course, and persevere to the last mile. These may be low-profile leaders with seemingly little power in the marketplace, but if they have influence with God, He will provide whatever influence they need with men.

Hindrances

Consider these hindrances to community transformation.

Theological misconceptions of revival. Often, we are the biggest obstacles, believing that community transformation is neither possible nor biblical. The Bible, however, says we are to humble ourselves, pray, seek his face, and turn from our wicked ways. Scripture says, *"If my people, who are called by my name, will humble themselves and pray and seek my face and turn from their wicked ways, then will I hear from heaven and will forgive their sin and will heal their land"* (2 Chronicles 7:14). We need to labor together with God for community transformation.

Reliance on programs. Programs are practical actions, ways of putting legs and feet to the vision God wants us to accomplish.

Planning and programs are never the end game; they are means to the end. When programs become the focus, they limit God's leading, resulting in religious hindrances rather than spiritual change.

The opening verses of Acts chapter six, where the early church leaders solved the food distribution problem, give us one example of planning and programs in keeping with God's will. What we want to avoid is putting new wine into old wineskins. With time, many of our programs become old wineskins.

Lowered expectations. We routinely lower the bar, settling for less than God wants us to do. Some of this comes from our tendency to self-reliance—not expecting God's supernatural power and intervention.

Misplaced motives. We must allow God to check our motives. He is our King, not simply a solution to our problems. God will respond to a pure heart—something we gain by seeking an intimate relationship with Him.

Ignorance of the past. Researching the history of the community enables us to repent for its atrocities, broken covenants, and past inequities. It is important to dissolve ungodly covenants and to get rid of practices that offend God.

No sense of membership. We need to recognize our need for each other. We have said that unity is a byproduct of relationships: those relationships begin with reconciliation and humility.

Lack of hunger. Many of us want God's presence. The problem is that we want it on our terms and only in our time slots. Our daily lives are too busy, leaving no time for God. If our norm is **not** to walk in intimate relationship with God, we cannot expect to see community transformation.

Revival is born out of passion. It requires walking in an intimate relationship with God to fulfill our destiny. Transformation is not the work of man, but the finger of God. It is time to seek the Lord!

(Adapted from The Sentinel Group. The Quickening. 2003. www.TransformNations.com)

Reflection and Discussion

1. What does a transformed workplace look like?

2. What does it mean when God says in Psalm 2:8, *"Ask of me, and I will make the nations your inheritance"*?

3. What can you do to change the structure and environment at work?

4. How can you be proactive to make a difference in your community?

5. What are you doing as a group to make an impact in the community?

6. Pray and ask God for the faith to see your city's entire marketplace transformed.

Activity

- Show "Transformation I" video. The Sentinel Group, 1999. www.TransformNations.com

- Show "The Quickening" video. The Sentinel Group. 2003. www.TransformNations.com

CHAPTER 10

BRINGING IN THE HARVEST

I have never seen the activity of God as great as it is right now in the workplace.—Henry Blackaby

The most common self-inflicted put-down is "I am not a pastor—I am just a layperson." This is all part of a clever satanic scheme to neutralize apostles, prophets, evangelists, pastors and teachers along with the entire army of disciples, already positioned in the marketplace.
—Ed Silvoso, Anointed for Business

Many believe that the next worldwide spiritual harvest will occur in the marketplace as God uses workplace ministers to bring revival. As in previous revivals, it will happen outside the walls of the church.

Past

The lay interdenominational prayer-based revival started in 1857. This began after the Second Great Awakening (1798-1832). It started in New York and spread across the country because of the faithfulness of a person in the marketplace. Jeremiah Lanphier, a Manhattan businessman from a Dutch Reformed Church, and six other businessmen began a noonday prayer meeting near Wall Street on September 23, 1857. Within six months, ten thousand people in New York's workplaces were praying every lunch hour for a mighty move of God.

Other cities followed the pattern. Soon, a common mid-day sign on business premises read, "We will re-open at the close of the prayer meeting." There were similar reports from all over the nation, from New York to California, Florida to Maine. Every segment of the marketplace felt the impact—businessmen, judges, students and housewives. Believers across the nation prayed and people filled the churches. This movement, begun in the business community, resulted in the greatest spiritual awakening in America, with more than one million people added to the church.

Present

Many believe that this kind of revival is beginning today. Henry Blackaby recently wrote, "…in the Bible, most of the activity of God that changed society was done in the workplace and not in the church…I believe it is the choice of God." The news media is noting that there is a great shift in interest toward spirituality in the workplace. Christians, however, must ensure that this movement focuses on Christ and not just new-age teaching or other cults.

Many believe that the final revival, the one predicted in Joel 2:28-32 and quoted by Peter in Acts 2:17-21, will happen in the workplace. *"In the last days, God says, I will pour out my Spirit on all people. Your sons and daughters will prophesy, your young men will see visions, your old men will dream dreams…everyone who calls on the name of the Lord will be saved."*

Relationship Between Work and the Great Commission

The workplace is ideally suited to the Great Commission. In Matthew 28:18-20, Jesus told his disciples: *"All authority in heaven and on earth has been given to me. Therefore go and make disciples of all nations, baptizing them in the name of the Father and of the Son and of the Holy Spirit, and teaching them to obey everything I have commanded you. And surely I am with you always, to the very end of the age."* This Scripture relates to the workplace in many ways.

- *"All authority in heaven and on earth has been given to me."* God has already given His followers in the marketplace His authority and jurisdiction in schools, businesses, and government circles. It is under His authority and power, both in the physical and spiritual realms, that they are able to influence their coworkers. Their job, as God's ambassadors in the workplace with all of the resources He has given them, is to make the greatest possible contribution to everyone within their influence.

- The assignment is to "*go,*" which in the original Greek translation means "having gone." Christians operating in the workplace have already gone and are already strategically positioned in the city.

- The task is to "*make disciples.*" Because workplace Christians daily make contact with a multitude of people, they have a ready platform from which to influence unbelievers during a normal workday. Living a Christ-like lifestyle in the workplace includes demonstrating love and concern for others, honesty, integrity, punctuality, joy, and clear, consistent priorities. Actions speak much louder than words.

- The target is "*all nations* (ethne)." Throughout the world, the marketplace is the center of society, the focal point of the city.

- A component of the task is "*baptizing*" them. We are to share the message of salvation with them.

- We are to teach them "*to obey everything commanded.*" Our place of work is ideal for teaching biblical principles and mentoring our fellow workers and employees. We can bring the gospel of the Kingdom to them on a daily basis.

- The promise is "*I am with you always.*" Workplace ministers share in the promise God gave Joshua: *"I will give you every place where you set your foot"* (Joshua 1:3).

The entire world has been entrusted to us. Mark records the Great Commission in these words: *"Go into all the world and preach the good news to all creation"* (Mark 16:15). Our focus is not just a church building or a gathering of believers. Our focus is to penetrate every sphere of influence—globally!

We are blessed to be a blessing. We are already blessed, but we need to look for ways to be a blessing. God blesses workplace Christians as they bless their co-workers. God blesses businesses as they are a blessing to their employees, suppliers, and city—just as He promised Abraham: *"I will make you into a great nation and I will bless you; I will make your name great, and you will be a blessing. I will bless those who bless you, and whoever curses you I will curse; and all peoples on earth will be blessed through you"* (Genesis 12:2-3). In Galatians 3:8, Paul reiterated God's promise to Abraham. *"All nations will be blessed through you."*

Workplace Ministers Are Positioned to Bring in the Harvest

"The harvest truly is great, but the laborers are few" (Luke 10:2). We need to ask ourselves: Why are we short of workers? Do they simply not exist or are they available but not equipped and released? Could it be that God has raised up an entire army of workers that is not being sent to the front lines?

The labor shortage can be solved easily by releasing workplace Christian leaders already strategically positioned to bring in the harvest. Compare this to a sports team. All members of the team are trained and equipped on the practice field to play the game. At game time, however, the majority sit on the bench, never playing in the real game. They must first be released, sent in by the coach to play the real game.

Workplace and Church Ministers Working Together to Reach a City

If we add up all the numbers that all Christian ministries claim as converts, the world has already been saved. But not only does the world not act like it, we know that a majority have not yet been evangelized. What is the problem? Where are all the converts?

The Parable of the Sower in Matthew chapter 13 sheds light on the problem. The chart below indicates the cause of failure of evangelistic efforts. While we could say that the devil is always the enemy behind our failure, it is clear that in two out of three of the failures, he uses the prevailing culture.

Every culture provides its negative influences. In the Third World, culture threatens survival. The stony ground of struggling to survive causes rootless, immature responders to withdraw. In the Western World, culture entertains. The thorny bushes of lust of the flesh and cares of life smother the clear call of the Gospel.

Seed Sown	*Results*	*Enemy*
Some fell by the wayside and the birds got them.	No positive response	Devil
Some fell on *stony* ground and had shallow roots.	Shallow, emotional response without true understanding of the Kingdom. Misplaced over-enthusiasm brings disappointment and leads to searching for another answer.	Culture
Some sprang up and the *thorns* choked them out.	Seem to have a genuine response, but something more important demands their attention. Wrong priorities lead to starvation.	Culture
Some fell on good soil and brought forth 100, 60 and 30 fold.	These transformed followers produce fruit as their new relationship with God compels them to share the Good News with others.	

Workplace and church ministers working together can nurture the seed that makes a start but is threatened by culture. This seed requires discipleship to survive. When workplace ministers remove rocks and thorns, the success rate of church ministers increases dramatically.

In the last chapter, we mentioned that a reliance on programs can hinder transformation, but we also pointed out that programs can be ways of putting legs and feet to the vision God wants us to accomplish. Consider these options for making an impact on the culture—programs that could help us nurture and harvest more seed: creating uplifting, morally encouraging, and spiritually challenging movies; creating games and family entertainment complexes based on biblical values; praying and working toward inventions that will transition wealth to the Christian community; developing educational curricula that will motivate believers to excel in leadership positions; creating investment opportunities and jobs in the Third World to raise the standard of living. The marketplace is the center of society, and efforts to reach cities must include the workplace.

Mel Gibson is an example of a workplace Christian who used his talents in the marketplace to make a tremendous impact. He repeatedly emphasized the fact that he felt called by God to bring *The Passion of the Christ* to the big screen. He said, "I'm not a preacher, and I'm not a pastor. But I really feel my career was leading me to make this movie. The Holy Spirit was working through me on this film, and I was just directing traffic. I hope the film has the power to evangelize. Everyone who worked on this movie was changed. There were agnostics and Muslims on [the] set converting to Christianity."

The Five-fold Ministry Inside and Outside the Church

The five-fold ministry gifts inside the church have equivalents in the workplace. God gifted the church with various kinds of leaders for its birth and operation, *"It was he who gave some to be apostles, some to be prophets, some to be evangelists, and some to be pastors and teachers, to prepare God's people for works of service, so that the body of Christ may be built up"* (Ephesians 4:11-12).

In the same way, He has given the workplace various kinds of leaders for its management. The following chart illustrates the parallels between church and workplace leaders in terms of their gifting.

Strong organizations have properly gifted people in the right positions. They determine through testing and observation what gifts a person has, deploying that person accordingly. Startup organizations require the gifts of apostle and prophet. The gift of teaching is needed to maintain product and service quality. The gift of evangelism is needed for strong sales and recruiting.

In the Old Testament, Joseph is typical of an apostle in government business. Daniel functioned as a prophet called to fulfill his ministry in the political field. In fact, more than 90 percent of the prophets never functioned inside the walls of the temple. The apostles and prophets ministered largely in the marketplace and public square.

Gifting	*Workplace Function*	*Function Description*
Prophets	Entrepreneur, Visionary, Analyst, Accountant, CFO	Many prophets are entrepreneurs and bold visionaries. Their analysis tends to be a confident black and white. They anticipate the outcomes of decisions as well as potential problems.
Apostle	Builder, Creator, Manager, Implementer	Apostles build the prophet's vision. They tend to be problem solvers, whether in the overall design of the organization, a division, or a product line. Apostles are good organizers, seeing what needs to be done on an operational level or with specific systems.
Evangelists	Marketer, Salesperson, Recruiter, Public Relations	Evangelists communicate the message. They influence customers, strategic partners, and employees. They have charisma, making people want to hear what they have to say.
Pastors	Human Resource Manager, Workplace Chaplains	Pastors deal with people internally, caring for their needs and helping them grow. Encouraging and sympathetic, they nurture employees.
Teachers	Production Supervisors, Department Heads, Professors, Technicians, Operations Manager, Quality Control	Teachers train others how to do their work. They understand how things function and are able to communicate with clarity and simplicity as they impart their knowledge to fellow employees.

Paradigm Shifts

A major harvest in the marketplace will require various paradigm shifts. Some of these shifts have already occurred, some are in process, and some are still to come.

Paradigm Shifts That Have Occurred

- Most believers now accept that there is one Church with many congregations. There is one Chief Shepherd, Jesus, and many undershepherds.
- Cities can and must be reached.
- Prayer is not just private, but also public—a key to revival.
- Through prayer we are able to change the spiritual climate of a city or region. *"I urge, then, first of all, that requests, prayers, intercession and thanksgiving be made for everyone—for kings and all those in authority, that we may live peaceful and quiet lives in all godliness and holiness"* (1 Timothy 2:1-2).

Paradigm Shifts in Process

- More people are realizing that there is not a division between clergy and laity.
- There is a growing awareness that truly loving the lost is an essential part of loving God. *"Jesus replied: 'Love the Lord your God with all your heart and with all your soul and with all your mind.' This is the first and greatest commandment. And the second is like it: 'Love your neighbor as yourself'"* (Matthew 22:37-39).
- Corporations are more accepting of faith expressed at work.
- There is a growing awareness that intercession is not a gift given to a few but something in which all Christians should be engaged (1 Timothy 2:1-8).
- More people are seeking restoration and forgiveness through repentance. Identificational repentance identifies with those

who have been sinned against and repents for the injustice done to them. This repentance takes responsibility for corporate sins and their consequences.

- Pastors are realizing their need to pastor the city as well as their congregation.

Paradigm Shifts to Come

- Faith to believe that God not only saves individual souls but also has the power to intervene and transform cities and nations: we need faith to believe that God wants to move and interact on a different level.

- A change in our focus from a salvation message of evangelizing souls to a Kingdom of God message of discipling cities and nations.

- The need to see churches as "equipping centers" that support workplace ministers in their calling.

- A stronger impact of prayer in the workplace. *"...The earnest prayer of a righteous person has great power and wonderful results"* (James 5:16 NLT). Cities are transformed when those who are in authority become passionate about their faith at work, because earnest prayer requires passionate faith.

- Increased awareness that revival can be ignited in the workplace.

- An understanding that we as Christians are the light of the world, that we are sent into the marketplace to penetrate it.

- A recognition of the authority—and its power in the marketplace—that Christians have in the name of Jesus.

- The entire church pastoring the entire city. Joel's prophecy quoted by Peter (Acts 2:17-21) will become a reality. The church will not be confined within the walls of its buildings. Both pastors and marketplace ministers will be motivated to fulfill the Great Commission (Matthew 28:18-20).

Reflection and Discussion

1. What are some ways we can remove the rocks and thorns?
2. What paradigm shifts need to occur for revival to happen?

CHAPTER 11

BUILDING THE KINGDOM

*You have planted much, but have harvested little…Give careful thought
to your ways… My house, which remains a ruin, while each of you
is busy with his own house… Build [my] house, so that I may take
pleasure in it and be honored... I am with you, declares the Lord.*
—Haggai 1:6-13

Workplace ministry is not a new concept. Throughout the Bible
there are many examples of church ministers and workplace ministers
working together to fulfill God's purpose of redeeming mankind and
building His Kingdom. God's wisdom in the structure of Israel can
help us in the New Testament church today.

Priests and Kings Function Together in the Old Testament

*A divine teamwork coexisted for centuries in Israel. Priests and
kings held two distinct offices with unique functions: priests provided
the vision and kings provided the provision.*

God selected the tribe of Levi to be His priests. The remaining
eleven tribes were the warriors, the providers, and the protectors of the
nation. There were approximately 27 men tithing for every priest. If
the Levites had tried to take all the committed men of Israel to make
priests out of them, they would have upset the balance between vision
and provision.

Priests carried the responsibility of hearing from God. They offered
sacrifices for the people, received tithes and offerings, and cared for

the house of God. Additionally, they cared for widows, orphans and strangers at the gate. They spoke encouragement to the people before battle.

Kings battled and destroyed the enemy. They took the spoils of war. Without the battle success of kings, priests would have nothing to distribute to bless the nation. Kings paid tithes and offerings to the priests. They governed the physical affairs of the nations.

Kings were not to go to war without the priest's blessing. *"When you are about to go into battle, the priest shall come forward and address the army. He shall say: 'Hear, O Israel, today you are going into battle against your enemies. Do not be fainthearted or afraid; do not be terrified or give way to panic before them'"* (Deuteronomy 20:2-3).

If a king tried to do a priest's job, he suffered judgment from the Lord. Saul's impatience to go into battle led him to step over the line. Samuel, the priest, was to make a burnt offering before battle. When Samuel was late, Saul offered the burnt offering himself, usurping the office of the priest. Samuel arrived shortly after and said to Saul, *"What have you done?"* (1 Samuel 13:11). Samuel pronounced words of judgment against Saul: "*You have not kept the command the Lord your God gave you; if you had, he would have established your kingdom over Israel for all time. But now your kingdom will not endure"* (1 Samuel 13:13-14).

Kings and the priests respected the anointing and calling of God on their respective offices. They shared both mutual need and mutual respect. When King David sinned with Bathsheba, Nathan, the prophet, came to him with a word of judgment (2 Samuel 12:1-15). David heeded Nathan's message and repented.

Old Testament: Priest and King Build the House of the Lord

The book of Haggai is about Joshua, a priest, and Zerubbabel, a governor, working together to rebuild the temple. Its principles apply to us today in suggesting how church and workplace ministers should prioritize working together to build the Kingdom. God reveals surprising blessings for rebuilding His house and negative consequences of neglecting His house (or work). See the end of this section for a diagram of the book of Haggai.

The first chapter describes how God used the prophet Haggai to call Zerubbabel and Joshua together to build the "house of the Lord." The Lord told them to give careful thought to their current ways. The people had been so focused on their own worldly needs that they had neglected God's house; they were living in luxurious paneled houses while the Lord's house remained in ruins.

God said, *"You have planted much, but have harvested little. You eat, but never have enough. You drink, but never have your fill. You put on clothes, but are not warm. You earn wages, only to put them in a purse with holes in it"* (Haggai 1:6).

After diagnosing their condition, God promises that He will "*be with them*" and "*bless them*" if they get their priorities right and work together to rebuild His house. He even promises that He will *"shake all nations,"* bringing those whom He desires, and that He will come and *"fill this house with glory"* (Haggai 2:7).

Haggai closes the book with God telling him to make a remarkable prophecy and promise to Zerubbabel, a marketplace leader. *"I will make you like my signet ring, for I have chosen you"* (Haggai 2:23). The signet ring was a sign or promise of hope for the full restoration of God's covenant people. The full weight of a king's authority accompanied any command sealed in wax bearing the imprint of the king's signet ring. Today, the Holy Spirit empowers workplace leaders to act as the imprint of God's signet ring, doing God's business with His authority and power.

(See the diagram from the Book of Haggai on building the house of the Lord on page 87.)

New Testament: Church and Workplace Ministers Function Together

One example, described more fully in chapter eight of this book, has the apostles commissioning workplace believers to manage a problematic food distribution system. See chapter eight for additional examples.

Church and Workplace Ministers Are Still Called to Function Together

Today, God is calling church and workplace ministers to work together to bring revival, transform our cities, and fulfill the Great Commission. Their combined time, effort, and finances are needed to build the Kingdom of God. His blessing, presence and glory still accompany those who are obedient—just as in Haggai's day.

Workplace ministry leaders who have been equipped and released by church ministers are to be like the signet ring of Christ, representing Him and His authority in the marketplace. The result will be the coming of a great harvest.

There is a natural progression for Kingdom building through community transformation.

1. Church and workplace ministers partner as peers with the focus of establishing God's Kingdom in the community.

2. Church ministers validate the call of workplace ministers, equipping and releasing them to change their workplace.

3. Workplace ministers passionately seek God to transform their workplaces in order to change the community.

Reflection and Discussion

1. How does the relationship of priests (church ministers) and kings (workplace ministers) play out in today's world?

Book of Haggai: Priest and Governor Building the House of the Lord

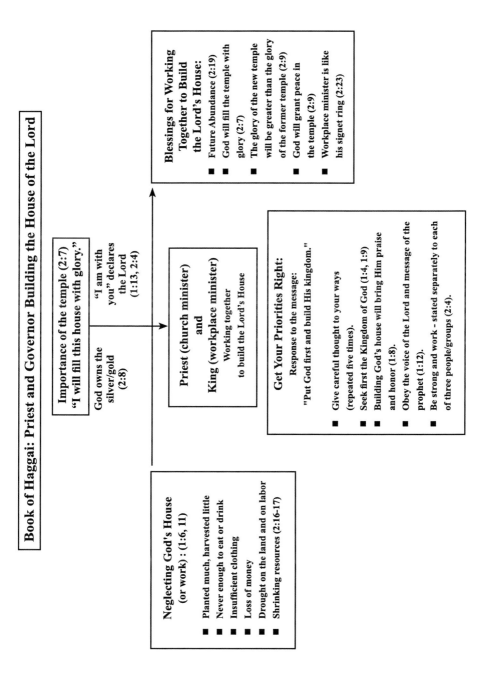

Importance of the temple (2:7)
"I will fill this house with glory."

God owns the
silver/gold
(2:8)

"I am with
you" declares
the Lord
(1:13, 2:4)

**Blessings for Working
Together to Build
the Lord's House:**

- Future Abundance (2:19)
- God will fill the temple with glory (2:7)
- The glory of the new temple will be greater than the glory of the former temple (2:9)
- God will grant peace in the temple (2:9)
- Workplace minister is like his signet ring (2:23)

**Priest (church minister)
and
King (workplace minister)**
Working together
to build the Lord's House

Get Your Priorities Right:
Response to the message:
"Put God first and build His kingdom."

- Give careful thought to your ways (repeated five times).
- Seek first the Kingdom of God (1:4, 1:9)
- Building God's house will bring Him praise and honor (1:8).
- Obey the voice of the Lord and message of the prophet (1:12).
- Be strong and work – stated separately to each of three people/groups (2:4).

**Neglecting God's House
(or work) : (1:6, 11)**

- Planted much, harvested little
- Never enough to eat or drink
- Insufficient clothing
- Loss of money
- Drought on the land and on labor
- Shrinking resources (2:16-17)

CHAPTER 12

WORKPLACE MINISTER AND CHURCH MINISTER RELATIONSHIP: CHALLENGES AND OPPORTUNITIES

Many church leaders are training us to do their ministry,
instead of our ministry.—Dr. Myles Munroe

Role confusion can cause discomfort in any relationship—even among committed believers. Every role carries with it a set of expectations, behaviors that are appropriate to its function. When roles are not clearly defined, unmet expectations are sure to follow. This is one of the biggest challenges facing workplace ministers and church ministers. This chapter helps to strengthen those relationships, enhancing their ability to advance the Kingdom.

Frustrated Workplace Ministers

Workplace ministers have expressed some frustrations in their working relationship with church ministers.

Many workplace ministers feel they are second-class citizens compared to those who serve in a church. They believe that their work is seen as secular and worldly. They sometimes feel that they are not involved in "real" ministry, that they are neither valuable nor necessary to God's plan. Unfulfilled workplace ministers risk becoming spectators because they can't find their place in the church. John Beckett, business leader and author of *Loving Monday* writes:

For years, I thought my involvement in business was a second-class endeavor—necessary to put bread on the table but somehow less noble than the more sacred pursuits like being a minister or a missionary. The clear impression was that to truly serve God, one must leave business and go into "fulltime Christian service." The majority of business people feel this way.

Workplace ministers sometimes feel guilty because of weak faith and an attachment to worldly things. Even though some workplace ministers know they have a call to ministry, they hesitate about exchanging their secular setting for a religious one. They feel like spiritual failures because they are not in "full-time Christian service." Ed Silvoso writes:

I always felt good about my job except when I was in church. Some well-meaning but totally misguided leaders looked down on my occupation. They would say to me, "When are you going to go into the ministry? You don't live by faith but by sight. At work you hang around sinners, people who drink and smoke. You have a calling on your life. Do not be rebellious. Leave everything and go into the ministry."

Many workplace ministers feel put down, isolated, neglected, and confused. When church ministers describe the call of God on their own lives, they often make it sound like the highest calling. Either subtly or not so subtly, they may refer to workplace ministers as untrained and uneducated.

Spiritually zealous workplace ministers are often encouraged by their pastors to go to Bible school or become directors in the church. When this happens, the workplace minister may misinterpret his kingly calling as a priestly calling, settling for a less effective role than God designed for him.

Many workplace ministers are pressed into church responsibilities to the point of burnout. They feel the pressure of church expectations, almost as if they were juggling the demands of two careers. Some pastors underestimate the difficulty of managing marketplace responsibilities, leading families, and trying to support all the ministries and programs of the church at the same time. As a result, workplace ministers often develop feelings of inadequacy and guilt in trying to live up to these expectations.

Some workplace ministers feel that they are only a source of tithing revenue. Some pastors have been guilty of viewing their workplace people as dollar signs, seeing them for what they can contribute to church programs instead of equipping them to use their gifts in the mission field of their workplace.

Workplace Christians are frustrated with the poverty mentality of the church. Many people in the church believe that poverty is a virtue. Whether from mistaken theology or simple envy, they can be very judgmental of a workplace minister with a financially successful business. The problem is bidirectional, however. Since the marketplace is motivated primarily by money, some workplace Christians may pressure the church to set an example of prosperity.

Many workplace ministers suffer from loneliness. They often lack regular fellowship with peers who understand their situation. Seeing themselves as spiritual POWs trying to survive with dignity in an environment that feels hostile to faith, they need the constant power and presence of God at work.

Workplace Christians often fail to rise to their God-appointed position. Workplace Christians underestimate the power of God in their workplace. Not recognizing their calling, they do not see their role in bringing transformation to their place of work.

Workplace Christians feel a lack of support. The lack of encouragement and validation from the church undercuts any vision of workplace transformation, leading many workplace Christians to ambivalence. Rather than realizing that they ultimately work for the Lord, they see themselves as merely working for a secular boss with secular ambitions. This cripples motivation, shifting spiritual initiative into neutral.

Frustrated Church Ministers

Church ministers have also expressed frustrations in their working relationship with workplace ministers.

Workplace ministers often seem uncommitted to the church. Pastors look for reassurance of their own performance by evaluating the level of commitment of their people. David High, author of *Kings and Priests*, states that "he couldn't answer the question, 'Committed to what?' It was the 'what?' that drove me to program after program to build a dynamic, explosive, successful and happy group of believers." Nothing seemed to work for this pastor as he tried to extract a high level of commitment in an arena he could see—various church programs—rather than that which he couldn't see—the workplace ministry.

Pastors feel frustrated that people in the workplace are not tithing. They feel that workplace ministers could and should release more of their money to support the church. As they watch workplace ministers accumulate wealth and build their financial enterprises, they wonder about a lack of commitment to invest in the work of the church. Even among tithers, pastors may sense an attitude that falls short of bringing their expertise into the church— an indication that they may feel no vested interest in its work.

One suggestion is to have people with moral authority in the church—those who believe in tithing and are gifted in giving— help to motivate workplace people. They can speak to workplace people, raising the vision for giving, teaching on budgeting, and instilling spiritual passion for giving. Crown Financial Ministries' small group studies have helped many churches turn this corner. Their new six-week program, *Business by the Book*, has also revolutionized the business lives of many workplace Christians.

Pastors are discouraged that most benevolent work is still done by the church. There has been too little involvement from workplace ministers partnering with the church as they did in Acts 6.

Church ministers are frustrated with the attitude of workplace Christians. They feel reluctance on the part of workplace Christians to be equipped and shoulder the responsibility of ministry, leaving all the work to pastoral staff.

Pastors fear that marketplace leaders will try to impose a business mentality on the church. Some workplace people have tried to get pastors to operate their churches like business corporations, using worldly techniques to accomplish spiritual purposes.

Pastors want involvement from their marketplace leaders but sometimes lack trust. Some marketplace leaders are arrogant, wanting to wield their power in the church as they would their business. In the absence of humility and clear lines of respect, pastors and even board members can feel bullied.

Pastors feel inferior and intimidated by organizational structure and power. Even though many pastors struggle with administrative problems, they are expected to be CEOs as well as shepherds. Many of them want neither the responsibility of nor the accountability for the administrative stuff. They want to be shepherds.

Pastors have difficulty deciding how to incorporate the new emphasis of workplace ministry into an already crowded schedule. Many pastors have not thought of people in the workplace as a high-priority emphasis. They fear the necessary adjustments in expanded vision, sermon preparation, and equipping programs.

Consequences of Poor Relationships between Workplace and Church Ministers

While workplace ministers and church ministers are not as polarized as they once were, they are not as close as they could be in the common pursuit of Kingdom goals. This situation results in some negative consequences.

The Church is not doing all that it is intended to do. Frustrated, guilt-ridden workplace Christians are trying their best to keep up with the unrealistic expectations of guilt-ridden pastors who create more and more programs.

The Church suffers from lack of long-range planning and provision. Church ministers scramble for the provisions required to support their vision. But when workplace Christians feel left out of the development of that vision, they take no ownership of it. They are often sensitive to the fact that when they generate provision without proper vision, the wealth can be wasted. *"Where there is no vision, the people perish"* (Proverbs 29:18 KJV). This results in what they perceive as a lack-of-vision crisis. Workplace Christians who have a love for God and a drive to produce wealth, yet have no church-centered vision, create their own vision.

Many churches are full of frustrated workplace leaders listening to frustrated church ministers who have heard from God but do not have the money to pursue their vision. Millions of dollars in provision are wasted when church ministers make poor financial decisions because they are not gifted in financial management. It is especially tragic when workplace leaders with strong gifts in that area are not consulted.

Many workplace Christians have watched the fiscal irresponsibility of the Church. They think, "How could I follow a pastor who says he hears from God and yet makes so many stupid decisions with God's money?" They withdraw their heart and stop giving. *"For where your treasure is, there your heart will be also"* (Matthew 6:21). Without the money from workplace Christians, church ministers can't fulfill their God-given desire.

Churches want their members' skills for the church's institutional life but rarely affirm them for ministry in the workplace. Churches seldom prepare these same people to live out their faith as they exercise their skills on the job. So what happens? Church members see the institutional church as having less and less relevance for their lives. Why bother to get very excited about somebody else's goals when they seem unconcerned with my needs and the place where I spend a third of my life—my work?

Community revival is delayed. Without cooperation to complete the work of the church in the community, we will never see our cities and nation transformed. Larger church buildings and more benevolence programs are not going to get the job done.

Both groups suffer from incomplete financial wisdom. While serving as business department chair at Eastern Mennonite University, John W. Eby conducted a survey, finding that only 9.4 percent of the businesspeople in his community would consult their pastors in dealing with financial difficulties. Pastors ranked ninth, behind "no one" in response to the survey—even when the financial questions included ethical issues. There are understandable reasons for this.

- Pastors and businesspeople often have basic differences in worldview. Some of their values are not measurable by the same yardstick. Pastors tend to focus on Kingdom values whereas business people focus on profit/loss statements.

- Pastors may be more comfortable with "process," and businesspeople with "measurable results."

- Pastors with a concern for biblical justice may speak the language of "wealth redistribution." Businesspeople with a concern for justice may speak of "wealth creation."

- Businesspeople may disdain the dependency generated by "charity," preferring instead to alleviate poverty through the use of "productive capital."

- Pastors are often accused of not understanding the role of capital, return on risk, and the pressure of meeting payroll in a competitive economy. Businesspeople are accused of being unsympathetic to those who can't make money.

Benefits of Good Relationships between Workplace and Church Ministers

The potential benefits of a good working relationship between workplace ministers and church ministers are enormous—probably beyond comprehension. There is a treasure of wisdom to be tapped, starting at a grass roots level.

If workplace ministers would be equipped, blessed, and commissioned to work for the Kingdom, they would view their work as having real purpose. When workplace ministers feel respected by church ministers, they are more committed to them and of more benefit to the church.

Affirmation by pastors is important to workplace ministers. Pastors naturally excel at spiritual input, and workplace ministers at organizational input. Clear roles and a clear line of demarcation needs to be established. Both need to come together in humility and respect for each other.

When workplace Christians are brought on board as ministry peers, problems that have frustrated pastors for years are often solved in a few days. Efficiency is an absolute must in the marketplace; workplace people bring this God-given talent to the church.

Workplace people can influence outsiders to connect with a local church. Most church leaders today have very little interaction with unbelievers. Without personal contact and interaction to overcome the unfair bias of the entertainment industry, many unbelievers hold to an image of the church that is an unfortunate caricature. Personal contact makes all the difference, and workplace leaders have it on a daily basis.

Teamwork creates more powerful, more effective churches that can minister in a more relevant way to their communities and to the world. Churches could provide chaplaincy to organizations. People in the workplace could provide resources for congregations. Church ministers and workplace ministers working together in their respective gifts and callings are vital to societal transformation and building the house of the Lord.

Connecting Workplace Ministers to Church Ministers

Traditional pastors are already recognized as ministers. The challenge is acknowledging and integrating workplace ministers as co-laborers. This requires the resolution of three major issues: differences in worldview, expected levels of involvement, and need for intentional reconciliation.

Worldview is the grid through which a person sees and processes the reality in which he lives. Both church ministers and workplace Christians need to broaden their worldview. Church ministers tend to see society through a vertical theological grid that is less connected to the horizontal dimension of everyday situations. Workplace Christians tend to see theology as something isolated that does not necessarily affect every social component in a practical and tangible way.

The *levels of involvement* for integrating workplace Christians with church ministers are *participation*—characterized by regular attendance; *partnership*—characterized by shared decision-making and responsibility; and *leadership*—characterized by full ownership and responsibility. The church should recognize these levels and encourage growth from participation to leadership.

There is a need for *intentional reconciliation* between church ministers and workplace ministers. We suggest the following steps to eliminate the spiritual deadlock.

1. Pastors need to affirm the biblical legitimacy of workplace Christians in the expansion of the Kingdom.
2. Pastors need to reach out and extend the right hand of fellowship to workplace Christians.
3. Pastors need to work together with workplace Christians and fully integrate them into the mainstream of ministry.

It is time for leaders in the church and the workplace to sit down together and ask God to reveal His plan for transforming our cities and nations, bringing in the harvest, and building the Kingdom.

Workplace Ministers and Church Ministers as Partners

Workplace ministers and church ministers need to partner in a new model that would more effectively deal with current realities. There are many areas where the church can benefit by looking at the workplace. Likewise, there are many areas where the workplace needs to look to the church for answers.

Structure

In the New Testament, Jesus' new model called for change, inclusion, and breaking down barriers. Organizations today are exploring and writing about new ways to organize and lead. As we evolve toward flatter management structures with power in the team rather than the individual, it is becoming increasingly difficult to distinguish the boss from the subordinate.

When Scripture speaks of leadership (1 Corinthians 12 and 1 Timothy 3), it is not the conventional CEO model adopted by many churches. The preferred leader is not one who wields power from the top but rather one who works with and for the faithful.

Today's churches are likely to see their pastor as a visionary who not only initiates but also implements the church's mission. Too many congregations put this load on the pastor, and too many pastors accept it.

Many organizations have learned that employees "down the line" are often most in tune with the needs and wants of customers. Could it be that church members are more in touch with the pulse of their communities and ways to meet their needs effectively?

Community

The workplace hungers for community and is a great deal more productive when it is achieved. There is a new management bumper sticker: "If you're not creating community, you're not managing." A core component of community is interdependence. This means being available to give and being willing to receive.

The irony is that while our churches are moving away from the New Testament model of community, marketplace organizations are embracing it. We need to create the community of the first century church. People are hungry for it; what better place to find it than in the church? After all, it was God's idea first.

Trust

All relationships are built on trust. And sound relationships are at the heart of business success. What Douglas McGregor said years ago still applies today: "Lack of trust at all levels curtails innovation and market opportunities."

The Christian community views trust as the foundation of a person's peace and freedom, the foundation for experiencing life. Trust promotes a healthy body, sustains relationships, builds a mature conscience, enables our spirit to worship, and allows people to become fully human and fully spiritual.

Love

The more value we place on our high-tech, information-drenched society, the more we need the flesh-and-blood interaction of caring individuals to convey love, acceptance and empathy. All the power in the world, if enacted outside of the faith community, is empty and futile. We are social beings created for companionship with a relational God.

Current organizational literature portrays the ideal leader as caring and respectful toward people, willing to share power. Rule by fear and domination are replaced by love. Peter Senge, in his book *The Fifth*

Discipline, talks about the need for "agape" love in the workplace, developing a commitment to serve one another. The best definition of love, he says, is the "full and unconditional commitment to another's completions." As marketplace Christians, we can bring Christ's "agape" love to those we serve in the workplace.

Sharing Power

It is human nature to hold on to authority and to centralize control. The divine model, however, empowers the powerless and involves others in the task of Kingdom building.

Jesus made it abundantly clear to his disciples that his concern was not to centralize power around himself but rather to empower others, to distribute authority and ownership to those who understood his message. The Great Commission is a prime example.

Servanthood

The towel and basin symbolize Jesus' ministry. "*...the greatest among you should be like the youngest, and the one who rules like the one who serves. For who is greater, the one who is at the table or the one who serves? Is it not the one who is at the table? But I am among you as one who serves*" (Luke 22:26-27).

No task was beneath him. But neither was there any doubt as to who was in charge. Voluntary servanthood demonstrates a strength of character that is contrary to conventional wisdom—but one that connects with the common person like nothing else. Jesus exuded this quality and it attracted a loyal following.

In the workplace, this same model applies. The servant leads by example and invites others to share in a vision that includes all and conveys a commitment to quality relationships. The leader is a servant who gently helps individuals to discover their own uniqueness and to find ways of attaching it to endeavors above and beyond themselves.   (Adapted from "Can Business and Church be Partners?" by Jim Smucker and Beryle Jantzi. www.hischurchatwork.com)

Reflection and Discussion

1. Why are some workplace ministers frustrated with church ministers?

2. Why are some church ministers frustrated with workplace ministers?

3. What are some consequences of a poor relationship between church and workplace ministers?

4. What are some benefits when pastors and workplace ministers relate as peers?

5. How can church ministers and workplace Christians connect and effectively work together?

6. Are you a church minister who has failed to see the calling that workplace people have received for the marketplace? If so, and begin relating to them in light of your new understanding.

7. Are you a workplace Christian who sees your church as an organization to be measured and managed by worldly standards? Do you expect the pastor to shoulder the burden of the ministry? If so, ask forgiveness and recognize God's call on both of you to fulfill His purposes together through your differing gifts and talents.

8. How can we help church ministers feel more comfortable in the marketplace, the place where many of their members experience their most significant social reality?

9. How can we encourage church ministers to get to know their members in the context of their work?

10. How can workplace Christians serve the church in addition to contributing money, serving on boards of trustees and building committees? For example, how might they assist in evaluating and motivating staff, coordinating resources, and setting goals?

Chapter 13

EQUIPPING

The function of the church is for the equipping of the saints for the work of service, to the building up of the body of Christ.
—*Ephesians 4:12 NAS*

Many people are frustrated at work because they do not have a biblical understanding of how God wants them to minister there. Even those who recognize their calling as workplace ministers may have difficulty knowing what to do, how to conduct their ministry at work. Equipping saints for ministry includes giving them that understanding.

Impart a Workplace Ministry Vision

Pastors need to help workplace ministers recognize their calling and anointing. God has anointed some believers specifically for the workplace. The Lord is in their hearts. The Holy Spirit is infusing their spirits. The Word is renewing their minds. They are ready.

What they desperately need is a pastor and the church body to acknowledge the calling and anointing God has given them for the workplace. They need help recognizing that Monday's ministry in the workplace is just as important as Sunday's ministry in church.

Pastors who show their congregations how to tie their dreams and talents together with Kingdom vision help them fulfill their life purpose. Every believer is called to do battle. Today's battlefield is the marketplace. When men and women catch the vision that they are going to war to do exploits for God, their new focus provides new energy. Nothing is more exciting or rewarding than tying into God's vision for us. When we accept Christ's invitation to take his yoke, we discover that being harnessed for the Kingdom naturally results in fulfillment.

Equip Workplace Ministers

The fourth chapter of Ephesians states the importance of equipping the saints for the work of service. Workplace Christians need to be specifically equipped for ministry in the workplace. *"It was he who gave some to be apostles, some to be prophets, some to be evangelists, and some to be pastors and teachers, to prepare God's people for works of service, so that the body of Christ may be built up until we all reach unity in the faith and in the knowledge of the Son of God and become mature, attaining to the whole measure of the fullness of Christ"* (Ephesians 4:11-13).

Work is not a side issue for some special interest group; it's an issue for the whole church. The vast majority of Christians work, with or without pay. They do it at home, in the "secular" workplace, at school—as either staff or students—and in other settings. The church should be concerned about the workplace because that is where people are. We are not suggesting that pastors work harder; many of them are already maxed out. But an adjustment in focus can make the same effort more effective in strengthening their people for the workplace.

The majority of our equipping for "ministry" has focused on what we do within the walls of the church. We have been equipping workplace ministers to do church programs rather than the ministry God has called them to do in the workplace. Successfully integrating faith life with work life must become a priority.

One church member expressed his feelings in these words: "I know God has created me for a unique purpose and called me for a special ministry, but I don't always sense that it is a ministry *at church*. I know God has given me spiritual gifts and I believe we should all contribute to our local church as well as to the broader

Kingdom. Sometimes I feel that my church spends more time equipping me to do *their* ministry than *my* life ministry. Don't they understand that I am an extension of them? I love my church and I really have a heart to serve. I want to understand and fulfill my purpose, my life ministry."

National research across denominations reveals these startling statistics.

- 55% of attendees have never heard a sermon on the subject of work.

- 75% have never been taught a biblical view of work.

- They generally feel that their churches do not support them meaningfully in their work; not in the preaching, teaching, worship, or pastoral care.

- When asked how helpful preaching and teaching was to various areas of their lives, respondents said that it was quite helpful in "personal spiritual issues" but less helpful for issues related to church life, less helpful still for issues related to home life, and not very helpful at all for issues relating to work life.

Today's believers clearly feel ill equipped for life, whether life at work or life at home. God is calling pastors and local churches to sharpen their focus on the real needs of workplace Christians. The longer-term payoff, even for programs inside the church walls, will be significant, far outstripping the investment.

Developing Workplace Leaders

"When you enter the land the Lord your God is giving you and have taken possession of it and settled in it, and you say, 'Let us set a king over us like all the nations around us,' be sure to appoint over you the king the Lord your God chooses. He must be from among your own brothers. Do not place a foreigner over you, one who is not a brother Israelite. The king, moreover, must not acquire great numbers of horses for himself or make the people return to Egypt to get more of them, for the Lord has told you, "You are not to go back that way again." He

must not take many wives, or his heart will be led astray. He must not accumulate large amounts of silver and gold. When he takes the throne of his kingdom, he is to write for himself on a scroll a copy of this law, taken from that of the priests, who are Levites. It is to be with him, and he is to read it all the days of his life so that he may learn to revere the Lord his God and follow carefully all the words of this law and these decrees and not consider himself better than his brothers and turn from the law to the right or to the left. Then he and his descendants will reign a long time over his kingdom in Israel" (Deuteronomy 17:14-20). Based on this Scripture, consider the following guidelines.

Workplace leaders have a God-given anointing. Workplace ministers must trust God to place them where He wants them to be so that they might always have His anointing upon them. Verse 18 makes a clear distinction between the king and the priest, but notice that they both use the same law—the Scriptures. *"When he takes the throne of his kingdom, he is to write for himself on a scroll a copy of this law, taken from that of the priests, who are Levites"* (Deuteronomy 17:18).

Workplace leaders need to know that their power is not in what they own (v. 16, 17). They need to look out for three things that the enemy routinely uses to bring them down: money, sex, and power. The Bible respectively refers to these in the following verses:

1. The king *"must not accumulate large amounts of silver and gold"* (v. 17).
2. The king *"must not take many wives, or his heart will be led astray"* (v. 17).
3. The king *"must not acquire great numbers of horses for himself, or make the people return to Egypt to get more of them"* (v, 16). *"Some trust in chariots, and some in horses, but we trust in the name of the Lord our God"* (Psalm 20:7).

They need to develop gratitude rather than greed, stewardship rather than ownership, an unwavering loyalty to God's Word, and a dependence upon God's strength rather than their own.

Workplace leaders are to know and obey the Word (v. 18-19). They need to have the Word of God in their hearts. *"...he is to read it all the days of his life so that he may learn to revere the Lord his God and follow carefully all the words...."* Workplace ministers need answers. They get their direction through time with the Lord and careful attention to His Word.

God-anointed workplace leaders serve in humility (v. 19-20). Pride is the father of all sin. God commanded that the king *"learn to revere the Lord his God and follow carefully all the words of this law and these decrees and not consider himself better than his brothers and turn away from the law..."*

Leaders constantly fight the temptation to think of themselves as above the law—as though some laws should apply only to the less enlightened. Even David, the king after God's own heart, stumbled over this in his arrogance with Bathsheba and her husband, Uriah.

Every leader needs to heed the warning of James: *"For where you have envy and selfish ambition, there you find disorder and every evil practice"* (James 3:16).

Obedience will result in tremendous blessings (v. 19-20). God rewards our obedience. He refuses to under-appreciate or under-reward our efforts to respond to His leading.

Equipping Topics for Workplace Ministers

In his famous story of the house built upon sand versus the house built upon rock, Jesus spoke of the need for proper foundations. Consider these foundations for workplace ministers.

Of utmost importance is a daily quiet time with God. Spending time with God is more important than spending time doing anything else. It is the single most powerful tool available to Christians in the workplace.

Develop a reverence for and submission to the Word of God and its principles. Many workplace Christians seem to believe that the Bible and its principles apply to Sunday but have little or no relevance at the workplace.

View prayer as an integral part of work. Workplace ministers need to pray for their fellow employees, customers, suppliers, and even their competitors. They should seek God for the provision of future employees and customers. They should seek His will for decisions, and they should give thanks publicly.

View the quality of products or services as a platform for testimony or ministry. God calls all of us to do the very best quality work we can. *"Whatever you do, work at it with all your heart, as working for the Lord, not for men…It is the Lord Christ you are serving"* (Colossians 3:23-24). His desire for excellence is in keeping with the gifts and abilities He has given. Instead of measuring us against an arbitrary standard, He wants us to be all He created us to be.

Be committed to personal spiritual growth. Leaders set the pace. They must model a commitment to growth if they want to see it in their organization. Accountability relationships feed the momentum of growth and help prevent long droughts. Good leaders model accountability, offering and receiving it without demanding it.

Trust God and give generously from the increase. "Trust" is an easy word to say—one simple syllable. So is "give." They just happen to be two of the most difficult commands to follow.

When Paul tells us in 2 Corinthians 9:7 that God loves a cheerful giver, he is talking about giving with gratitude. This kind of giving, neither grudging nor in greedy anticipation, requires trust. When people finally realize that God's will for them also happens to be in their best interest—their best possible future— they begin to live with open hands, experiencing His peace and joy.

Steward time, resources, and money. Work is a gift from God. Everything He entrusts to His children is given to them to manage for a time. As stewards of God's property, workplace ministers view every decision as a spiritual decision. They recognize the high value God places on simple faithfulness. *"And if you have not been trustworthy with someone else's property, who will give you property of your own?"* (Luke 16:12).

Strive to make work both profitable and purposeful. Work serves multiple purposes as it provides income, helps build character, increases influence, and gives a platform for ministry. John Wesley's three keys to financial success are: make, save, and give. "Make all you can, save all you can, and give all you can."

Surrender your life to God. Workplace ministers face the greatest challenge in life—daily surrender. That means getting their priorities right. They need to cultivate God's heart for bringing the lost into the Kingdom. Information is important; intelligence is more important; but integrity is essential.

Release Workplace Ministers

The church needs to release God's anointed workplace leaders by praying for and standing beside them. In Acts, the church leaders prayed over and released their workplace leaders. *"They presented these men to the apostles, who prayed and laid their hands on them"* (Acts 6:6).

Pastors must do the same thing today. God wants to use an army of marketplace people to spark transforming revival—to reach cities and nations for Himself.

Reflection and Discussion

1. What does equip mean?
2. Why do pastors not focus on equipping people to minister in the workplace where they spend most of their time?
3. How would you describe the danger of viewing church members exclusively in terms of their contribution to church programs rather than their contribution to Kingdom growth?

4. How might a local church be strengthened by its people ministering outside of the building?

5. Share what you know about a church that is equipping and releasing workplace ministers.

6. How can pastors specifically equip workplace ministers?

7. To what extent do you think marketplace Christians really want to be *all* God wants them to be?

8. At work, how do you demonstrate a respect for and submission to God's principles?

9. How does prayer play a role in your workplace? Is your prayer practice the same at work as it is at home?

10. At work, how do you show a concern for the lost?

11. If you are a business owner, does your business give in a way that represents your heart?

12. How do others see your faith evidenced in the quality of your work?

13. What are you doing to grow spiritually?

14. Describe the kind of spiritual accountability you currently have.

CHAPTER 14

SETTING APART AND COMMISSIONING

They presented these men to the apostles, who prayed
and laid their hands on them.
—Acts 6:6

The church needs to equip, anoint, and commission people in every sector of the marketplace. Just as church ministers are ordained in their calling to the church, mature, godly workplace leaders can be set apart, or commissioned, as fulltime ministers in the workplace. This helps to define their purpose, giving them a rite of passage and recognition for their work in the Kingdom.

Some churches actually ordain their members for ministry. Ordination confirms that they are in the ministry, that they have a clear call of God into the marketplace arena and are actively involved in influencing it.

This kind of commissioning and ordaining should not be confused with the ordaining of pastoral staff. It does not affect the workplace minister's legal status with IRS, nor does it satisfy denominational requirements regulating the performance of certain ministerial functions. This is a unique commissioning for a unique ministry.

Although this commissioning and ministry is unique to each individual's circumstances, it should not be unique in the sense of being rare. Ideally, most members of most churches should be ministering under this commissioning or be in the process of qualifying for it.

Biblical Support for Commissioning Workplace Ministers

The sixth chapter of Acts provides the clearest biblical example of commissioning workplace leaders. A problem surfaced in the food distribution program of the church—a problem that threatened its harmony and growth. The apostles recognized that they could not and should not be the ones to handle the distribution; their calling was to preach and pray. They needed to solve the problem through delegation, so they selected seven workplace leaders of proven ability and character, calling them to deal with this responsibility.

The apostles laid their hands on these seven workplace leaders recognized as being "full of the Spirit and wisdom," commissioning them to do the work. These men are referred to as "the Seven" in Acts 21:8. Many people refer to "the Seven" as deacons, but that word never appears in the Acts 6 text. Rather, they were known as spirit-filled workplace leaders.

Qualifications for Commissioning Workplace Ministers

The qualifications for commissioning workplace ministers mirror the criteria in Acts 6:3. The Amplified version uses these descriptors: *"men of good and attested character and repute, full of the [Holy] Spirit and wisdom."*

Acts 6:5 adds the words "full of faith and of the Holy Spirit" as it describes Stephen. Clearly, these men had earned good reputations, both in the workplace and in the community.

Imagine our churches filled with men and women aspiring to serve in this capacity. Imagine the influence they would be gaining in the marketplace as they work to earn a good reputation there. Imagine their impact within the church as they grow toward being "full of the Holy Spirit and wisdom." Is it any wonder that the early church was blessed with explosive growth and marketplace transformation?

Reflection and Discussion

1. What is your opinion about setting apart or commissioning workplace ministers?

2. Do you think it is possible to see a new explosion of marketplace transformation? If not, what would it take to change your opinion? If yes, what can you do to encourage it?

CHAPTER 15

SUPPORTING MINISTRY IN THE WORKPLACE

Workplace ministry will be one of the core future innovations in church ministry. —George Barna, Boiling Point, *Regal Publishing*

When the church begins to think about where people actually spend their time and the kinds of issues they face, it may begin to set a different agenda for its teaching and care. Supporting workplace ministers must become a high priority.

Issues in the Workplace

A recent study indicated that workers are working longer hours and suffering increasing levels of stress, anxiety and depression. This is not just a middle-class, white-collar phenomenon. Workers at every level are suffering as satisfaction with their jobs, their work relationships, their sense of purpose and significance are all in decline.

Americans, perhaps more than any other culture, define themselves by their work. For example, Americans work 2,000 hours per year, whereas Germans average 1,500 hours per year. If we assume a 40-hour workweek, it would mean that Germans have the annual equivalent of three months more personal time than the average American.

The church has an opportunity to help people not only collaborate with an increasingly oppressive system but also co-labor with God to transform it. The church needs to help people go beyond merely trying to cope. It can begin to challenge the excesses of contemporary capitalism and offer wholesome improvements.

Values of the Contemporary Workplace

To achieve a healthy integration between work and the rest of life, we need to look at the values that shape workplace life.

The first value is practical atheism. Contemporary workplaces assume that God does not intervene in the affairs of business, that they are not accountable to Him, and that He, in fact, does not exist. Even many Christians are afflicted with the disease of practical atheism as they discount God from the economic process. It is crucial for the church to remind workplace ministers that God can intervene and provide direction both in the boardroom and the bakery.

The second value is the idea that people equal function. One negative consequence of the Industrial Revolution is the tendency to dehumanize people, to commoditize them as functional solutions rather than individuals created in the image of God.

Other cultural factors aggravate this problem. The pace and mobility of American life result in superficial relationships and fleeting encounters as we mingle with more people in a week than most previous generations encountered in a lifetime. The average American changes careers three to four times and has 15 different jobs during his lifetime. As fewer people work in the same town they live in, the quality of relationships at work erodes even further, leading to a sense of indifference toward co-workers. The church must remind workplace believers to see co-workers through God's eyes.

The third value is individualism. Despite the popular rhetoric of "teamwork," the contemporary workplace, like the culture at large, is becoming increasingly individualistic. It is natural for an unhealthy independence to creep into the lifestyle of believers, cutting them off from the body of Christ and its wisdom, encouragement and prayers. Workplace ministry can become just one more thing people do on their own.

The fourth value is materialism and the problem of never enough. Money is the major incentive in most workplaces: money to fuel greedy consumption. Many employees are stricken with the attitude that more is better but never enough. The church can help workplace ministers prioritize their values so that materialism does not become their master. In the process, however, pastors need to be careful not to attribute materialistic motives to everyone who is working too many hours. For many, the choice is not between long hours and family time but between long hours and unemployment. We desperately need marketplace transformation.

The fifth value is equating work with worth. There is an unhealthy tendency for people to feel defined by their work, as though their careers create their identity. Believers are subject to the same temptation. This may, in turn, fuel a tendency to believe that we earn God's love by what we do for Him. The church must reinforce the truth that our worth comes not from our work but from our identity in Christ.

Convictions Needed by Workplace Ministers

For people to integrate work and faith, they need some basic convictions. Here are several.

Their work matters to God. God uses work not only to provide for physical needs but also to develop the character of His people, enabling them to influence others. Work done with the right attitude becomes an act of worship. It matters a great deal to Him.

They are called by God to the marketplace. Workplace ministers are not defined by their work but by their relationship to God and to other people. Their job or daily work is in no way inferior in God's eyes to the work of church ministers.

The workplace is a context for spiritual growth and for ministry. Ministry is not confined to the church building or retreat center.

They should expect the support of their brothers and sisters in Christ, wherever they are, whatever their work. In turn, they should extend similar support to other believers.

Work must not become an idol. It must be set within the overall context of God's command to rest and to meet responsibilities to family, friends and the body of Christ.

Supporting Workplace Ministers

Pastors need to help members function in their daily nine-to-five windows. They play a key role in infusing Kingdom principles into the marketplace. Supporting workplace ministers requires affirmation, understanding, and guidance. Consider these actions churches can take to help people integrate their faith and work:

Recognize God's presence in the marketplace. God is already present in the marketplace we want to reach. He is waiting for the church to join Him.

Focus on the life of the church beyond its walls. Christians have been sent to minister to the world. A large part of that world is the workplace.

See people's work as sacred rather than secular. Affirm workplace Christians in their call to workplace ministries. Pray regularly for them. Use the word "ministry" properly, with clear recognition that it includes ministry at work and in the community.

Equip people for workplace ministry. Recognize people in the workplace as the "front lines" of the church. What army would send soldiers to the front without training or weapons? What makes us think we can?

Encourage people to be lights in a dark world. In the Sermon on the Mount, Jesus said, *"Let me tell you why you are here. You're here to be salt—seasoning that brings out the God-flavors of this earth…You're here to be light, bringing out the God-colors in this world"* (Matthew 5:13-14 MSG).

Teach the basics of the faith as applied to the workplace. People who are strongly grounded in their faith are more effective in relating their faith to their work.

Create a biblical framework for work. Let people know that their work and their workplace matter to God.

Create and maintain faith consciousness at work. Encourage people to practice the presence of God in the workplace. Equip and encourage them to take initiative in prayer and action to see their workplaces transformed.

Stress the "priesthood of all believers." Reinforce the idea that we are all ministers of the gospel.

Listen to workers' needs and issues. Create opportunities to listen to people regarding their work-related issues. People have a lot to say about their work, but few are willing to listen. As you listen, you will learn the kind of support people need; it will become obvious. This may be the most important thing churches can do to help—especially at the beginning.

Relate to marketplace issues. Seek to hear and understand the current culture. Explore the marketplace issues that are relevant to people in the church. Encourage and support those who are prompted to take a stand on issues in their work environment.

Provide prayer and worship times that relate faith and work. Prayers of thanksgiving affirm a person's calling and service to the larger community. Specifically name the roles of teachers, managers, public servants, transportation workers, retailers, social workers, financial services workers, food servers, etc.—whatever exists in your church. Offer prayers of intercession for difficult situations such as downturns in business, strikes, disasters or other major challenges.

Getting Your Church to Work

Consider some ways a church can connect with its workplace ministers.

Plan to transform the church. The church must not view workplace ministry as an add-on option or a mere program offering. Workplace ministry must become part of the church's DNA, affecting how it speaks, equips, affirms and commissions its people.

Identify workplace issues by taking a survey at the church. The survey could ask:

- What is your job?
- What is your gender? (This is asked to identify gender-specific issues.)
- What are the issues you face at work?
- How might the church help you apply your faith in the context of daily work life?
- How can we pray for you in your area of work?

Ask workplace Christians from different vocations to give input on sermons that could address their needs.

Focus a percentage of sermons on the workplace. According to a recent study, work is among the subjects that sermons are least likely to address even though most members would like it addressed more often. The same study revealed greater satisfaction with their congregation among members when sermons addressed workplace issues. Consider these issues for relating sermons to workplace applications.

- Bring workplace issues into the normal flow of preaching and teaching subjects. Raise questions that will bring workplace issues into the text, e.g., What is the Kingdom of God and how can I bring it into my workplace?
- Teach on reconciliation, restoration, and propitiation in relation to how one can apply those principles at work, e.g., How can I increase the value of others?

- Teach on the value and purpose of work.
- Teach on the priesthood of all believers in the context of work.
- Teach on various workplace people: Lydia in the clothing trade, Daniel, Deborah or Joseph in government, Nehemiah and Ezra in construction, Priscilla and Aquila in affordable housing, Job and Jacob in agribusiness, and Matthew in finance.
- Teach on various themes and issues such as money, power, ethics, witness, management, service, and conflict.

Invite members to present a five-minute workplace testimony. Brief testimonies of integrating faith and work can have powerful benefits. They provide inspiration, perspective, encouragement, and a model for others to integrate faith and work as well as to talk about it.

Recognize ministry already occurring in the workplace. Recognition by church leadership heightens the visibility of ministry occurring beyond the church's walls, naturally encouraging others to follow the example. Members can share what they do for a living, how it helps people, and how they are able to minister through their occupation.

Develop small support groups. Small groups are crucial to workplace transformation, bridges between Sunday faith and weekday life. Creating safe places for people to develop accountability and regular support is enormously fruitful. A small support group is usually more effective than a large one because it is more intimate and focused.

Several good things happen as group members discuss living out their faith at work. They think in a more focused way, which adds depth. They hear additional perspectives, which often add clarity. They are inspired by stories of victories and encouraged by shared struggles.

When people know that the small-group agenda includes questions about their work, it raises their faith consciousness throughout the week, fueling prayer and action. The support of praying and strategizing together about making a difference in the workplace is a great benefit.

Specifically incorporate a workplace focus in mission and outreach activities. Coordinate various businesses to reach out into the community.

Help workers develop an Action Plan for Workplace Ministry. Encourage people to develop a ministry plan. (See the "Action Plan for Workplace Ministry" and "Plan for Workplace Transformation" chapters in this book.)

Set apart or commission workplace ministers. Affirm workplace believers through a formal commissioning service to recognize and confirm their calling. Lay hands on and pray for each workplace minister.

Engage the marketplace. Encourage pastors to visit church members in their places of work to better understand the struggles and opportunities of the workplace environment. In many cases, they can do leadership training or even discipleship within businesses.

Be a church "of" the community rather than a church "in" the community. Recognize that the church itself does business within the community. Build mutually beneficial relationships and alliances. Church members routinely encounter all kinds of people—salespeople, postal workers, repair people, etc.—all who need to experience the love of Christ personally.

Provide all members with the support base they need to do their ministry. All members can be church planters in their area of work. Ask them what types of resources would help them be successful, and then supply those resources.

Look for creative, biblical ways to reach the community with maximum effectiveness. Rather than just ministering in the church, think about how to minister to the community. Identify elements of the community that the church needs to address and then develop an intentional outreach strategy for each one.

Create an internet devotional ministry for workplace ministers.
Write your own devotional or subscribe to free meditations from
www.todaygodisfirst.com. Send them directly to members.

*Make members aware of web sites and ministries that
help them integrate their faith and work.* The following sites
contain articles, books and links to organizations that help
those in the workplace integrate their faith with their work.
www.todaygodisfirst.com, www.christatwork.com, www.
hischurchatwork.org, and www.marketplaceleaders.org.

Provide career counseling and employment assistance.
Career counseling and employment assistance offer significant
help to members. Churches can sponsor employment helps such
as a job-hunting and availability bulletin board, a care group for
unemployed or transitioning members, or internships for young
people at members' places of work.

*Post a "Servant's entrance" sign above every door leading
out of the church.* The signs are on the inside, precisely where
most buildings would have a sign saying "Exit." The signs bear an
important message: the real ministry of the church is not "in here"
but "out there."

Reflection and Discussion

1. Where is the church Monday through Friday?

2. Do our church members view themselves as agents of the
   Kingdom of God where they work?

3. How can a congregation better affirm and mobilize its pew
   sitters to minister within their jobs?

4. What would it look like if effectively prepared church members
   actually lived their faith at work?

5. What actions would they be taking to demonstrate their faith?

6. What would the churches be doing to prepare them?

CHAPTER 16

LAYING THE FOUNDATION FOR PLANNING

In his heart a man plans his course, but the Lord determines his steps.
—*Proverbs 16:9*

Many aspects of an envisioned future can be influenced or changed by decisions and actions you make today. For the Christian, this is not simply projection-based planning but the realization that through prayer and obedience you can be a catalyst to help bring about a future that is in alignment with God's will. Through prayer, the framework for a ministry action plan is established. Implementing the plan requires continued daily prayer for direction accompanied by obedient action in response to what God reveals.

One of the questions many Christians wrestle with is, "Should a Christian try to plan future direction?" James 4:14 (NASB) says, *"Yet you do not know what your life will be like tomorrow. You are just a vapor that appears for a little while and then vanishes away."* So why plan? The next verse goes on to say, *"Instead, you ought to say, 'If the Lord wills, we will live and also do this or that.'"* The real issue is not *whether* we should plan; it is whether we will put God's will first in our planning, always deferring to His wisdom and sovereignty.

Our attitude when we plan should result in this kind of prayer: "God, we want your will above everything else. We're not just asking you to bless whatever plan we devise—we want your wisdom. We want to move by your direction and in your timing. Please guide our thoughts and keep our hearts tuned to yours."

God designed us with the ability and need to plan. From the moment He placed Adam in the Garden "to work it and take care of it" (Genesis 2:15), planning became essential. If anything, it is even more important after the Fall. *"Be very careful, then, how you live—not as unwise but as wise, making the most of every opportunity, because the days are evil. Therefore do not be foolish, but understand what the Lord's will is. Do not get drunk on wine, which leads to debauchery. Instead, be filled with the Spirit"* (Ephesians 5:15-18).

These verses warn us not to be foolish, just doing what comes naturally with no life strategy. That results in weakness and missed opportunities to live for God in an evil environment. Planning is a necessity, helping us to be aware and make the most of the opportunities God provides. The key is to make plans by seeking God and asking for His discernment.

Assess Your Need for a Workplace Plan

- Do you know how God wants you to use your workplace position for the Kingdom?
- Do you know how to bring transformation to your workplace?
- Do you know what your workplace will be like in three years?
- Could you be more effective?
- Could your staff be more efficient?
- Could you have a greater impact for the Kingdom in your workplace?

A good plan coupled with appropriate action gives you traction to go from where you are to where God wants you to be!

A Scriptural Basis for Planning

God's Word Teaches that We Should Plan

"The plans of the diligent lead to profit" (Proverbs 21:5).
"Commit to the Lord whatever you do, and your plans will succeed" (Proverbs 16:3).

Planning Helps to Enable God's Best for Us

God wants only the best for his children. When we make Him the center of our planning, we free Him to give us His best. *"May he give you the desire of your heart and make all your plans succeed"* (Psalm 20:4).

Planning Means Anticipating Costs and Consequences

"The wisdom of the prudent is to give thought to their ways" (Proverbs 14:8). Prudent people know where they are going. Planning helps them get there. Every mistake revealed on a planning sheet saves the cost, pain and waste of the same mistake in real life.

A wise person calculates the hard and hidden costs. Luke 14:28-33 presents two parables that underscore the importance of counting the cost: the first is about building a tower. *"Suppose one of you wants to build a tower. Will he not first sit down and estimate the cost to see if he has enough money to complete it?"* (Luke 14:28). The second parable is about a king going to war. Jesus relates both stories to the cost of being His disciple, emphasizing the price to be paid and the necessity of counting the cost beforehand.

The cost of being a disciple of Christ is more than financial. Consider these additional costs as you plan.

- Will God be glorified by my actions?
- How will people react?
- How will people be affected?
- Is anyone likely to be offended or hurt by this?
- What resistance will I encounter?

- What effects will my plan have?
- What unintended effects might my plan have?

Planning Produces Favor

When God gives us understanding, we gain favor with man. *"Good understanding wins favor"* (Proverbs 13:15). People will see that we know where we are going and how to get there, that we know the costs as well as the consequences. Being diligent assumes planning, and those plans lead to plenty. *"The plans of the diligent lead to profit as surely as haste leads to poverty"* (Proverbs 21:5).

Planning Helps Us to Heed the Warnings in Scripture

The Scriptures warn us: *"Do not boast about tomorrow, for you do not know what a day may bring forth"* (Proverbs 27:1). *"Pride only breeds quarrels, but wisdom is found in those who take advice"* (Proverbs 13:10). Pride, as used here, means relying solely on our own opinion and not seeking God's wisdom or the counsel of others. This is human nature—the fallen nature that is in deadly rebellion to God's purposes.

A good planning process keeps us humble and constantly returns us to God for His perspective. While planning, we continually ask, "Lord, what is your direction in this area?"

Planning Can Keep Us from Disaster

Planning can keep us from doing what might seem right but would end up in disaster. We usually intend to do the right thing but we often fail to think through the whole process. After the disaster, our post-mortem evaluation reveals that we did not consider unintended consequences. *"There is a way that seems right to a man, but in the end it leads to death"* (Proverbs 14:12).

We need to be prudent, carefully considering our steps. *"A simple man believes anything, but a prudent man gives thought to his steps"* (Proverbs 14:15).

How We Should Approach Planning

Scripture teaches us the planning process. Consider these guidelines.

Plan by Seeking God's Wisdom

We begin the planning process by seeking what God wants us to accomplish. He reveals His desires through Scripture, inspired thoughts in our minds, and the counsel of others. He may also use dreams, visions, and prophecy.

The key is to meet with God, get our directions from Him, and then be obedient. There is no substitute for serious study of God's Word. The same is true for unhurried time in which we not only speak our concerns but also listen.

Look at the importance God places on wisdom.

"Teach us to number our days aright, that we may gain a heart of wisdom" (Psalm 90:12).

"The fear of the Lord is the beginning of knowledge, but fools despise wisdom and discipline" (Proverbs 1:7).

"He who walks with the wise grows wise, but a companion of fools suffers harm" (Proverbs 13:20).

"Christ, in whom are hidden all the treasures of wisdom and knowledge" (Colossians 2:3).

"But if you harbor bitter envy and selfish ambition in your hearts, do not boast about it or deny the truth. Such 'wisdom' does not come down from heaven but is earthly, unspiritual, of the devil. For where you have envy and selfish ambition, there you find disorder and every evil practice" (James 3:14-16).

Plan by Trusting God and Acknowledging His Leading

"Trust in the Lord with all your heart and lean not on your own understanding; in all your ways acknowledge him, and he will make your paths straight" (Proverbs 3:5-7).

Look at the three specific commands God gives us in this passage.

Trust in the Lord with all your heart. Trust must precede any honest request of God. Part of that trust comes to us as a gift from God, and part of it we learn through the experience of life. Our trust is not constant: it fluctuates as it grows in an overall upward direction. Although it is never complete, we deal with the deficiencies when we pray like the loving father in Mark 9:24, *"I do believe; help me overcome my unbelief!"* When we plan, it is absolutely necessary to trust God for guidance.

Do not lean on your own understanding. Our own understanding serves a purpose; God repeatedly instructs us to gain understanding and wisdom. But He realizes that our perspective is finite and imperfect, and that we must recognize the superiority of His perspective. When we devise a plan that violates His will, we must yield our wisdom to His. If He gives us a strategy that is unconventional and beyond our ability and understanding, again we must yield our wisdom to His. Such a strategy may require supernatural means; the Bible is filled with accounts of them.

In all your ways acknowledge Him. We acknowledge God's role as our master; we acknowledge that He will direct our paths; we acknowledge Him when we publicly give Him thanks for His goodness; we acknowledge Him—even in what appears to be failure—as we recognize that His agenda, even though it may be veiled for a time, is superior to our own.

Plan by Emphasizing Prayer, then Action

Since God's wisdom and direction are the only solid foundation for our plans, we need to continually ask, "What is the Lord saying?" It does no good, however, to ask that question if we are not committed to wholehearted obedience to whatever the answer is. Conditional commitment should never expect to be rewarded with clear direction. Our goal is seamless integration between God-led vision, God-inspired plans, and God-motivated action.

We need to move in faith to implement God's plan for us. This may be easy at the beginning, when we are still in the optimistic honeymoon phase of a plan. But then come the details. The old saying that the devil is in the details is a warning that we can expect Satan to attack us with fear, confusion and discouragement. We dare not retreat from a position of complete dependence on God. We never stop consulting Him, always subjecting our wills to His. We do not question in the dark what He has shown us in the light. We keep praying and we keep moving.

Plan with Balance: We Plan, God Directs

We do the planning and God does the directing. *"Look here, you people who say, 'Today or tomorrow we are going to such and such a town, stay there a year, and open up a profitable business.' How do you know what is going to happen tomorrow? For the length of your lives is as uncertain as the morning fog—now you see it; soon it is gone. What you ought to say is, 'If the Lord wants us to, we shall live and do this or that.' Otherwise you will be bragging about your own plans, and such self-confidence never pleases God. Remember, too, that knowing what is right to do and then not doing it is sin"* (James 4:13-17 TLB).

We plan. We begin by asking God to put His desires in our heart. Psalm 37:4 instructs, *"Delight yourself in the Lord and he will give you the desires of your heart."* As we delight ourselves in God, He puts His desires in our heart. When we want the same things He does, we can expect His blessing. Proverbs 16:9 reminds us that *"a man plans his course, but the Lord determines his steps."* Nehemiah is a good example of this principle. God put it in Nehemiah's heart to rebuild the walls, and Nehemiah planned how to do it.

God directs. What unfolds may be different than our original plan because of God's continuing direction. We plan to the best of our ability with God's help, trusting Him to direct our steps. Proverbs 19:21 reminds us, *"Many are the plans in a man's heart, but it is the Lord's purpose that prevails."*

Plan with Diligence

Planning is hard work. It can be mundane and boring. However, we must learn to be diligent because Satan will attempt to derail us. Consider these encouraging verses.

"The precious possession of a man is diligence" (Proverbs 12:27 NASB).

"Commit to the Lord whatever you do, and your plans will succeed" (Proverbs 16:3).

"May the favor of the Lord our God rest upon us; establish the work of our hands" (Psalm 90:17).

"The plans of the diligent lead to profit as surely as haste leads to poverty" (Proverbs 21:5).

Plan as Directed by God

God has created us to do good works. *"For we are God's workmanship, created in Christ Jesus to do good works, which God prepared in advance for us to do"* (Ephesians 2:10). This verse shows us God's advance preparation; He has specific works in mind. Our attitude as we plan should be, "Lord I want what you want. Please make me sensitive to your direction. Please stop me rather than allow me to waste effort on something you don't want."

Dead works are works produced through self-will and self-effort, the same will and effort shown by the Pharisees in their prideful and imperfect obedience to the law. If God gives us an idea and we run with it in our own effort, leaving Him out of the process, we create headache and heartache for ourselves and for those around us. That is why Hebrews 6:1-3 reminds us, *"Let us press on to maturity, not laying again a foundation of repentance from dead works..."*

Good works are the opposite of dead works; they are based on faith in Christ and the leading of the Holy Spirit—and they glorify God. The Apostle Paul teaches us about the difference by contrasting two types of building materials—wood, hay, and straw versus gold, silver, and costly stones. The wood, hay, and straw represent the self-directed "good stuff" we do on our own terms and for our own glory. The gold, silver, and costly stones represent God-directed good works, done for His glory.

> *"If any man builds on this foundation using gold, silver, costly stones, wood, hay or straw, his work will be shown for what it is, because the Day will bring it to light. It will be revealed with fire, and the fire will test the quality of each man's work. If what he has built survives, he will receive his reward. If it is burned up, he will suffer loss; he himself will be saved, but only as one escaping through the flames"* (1 Corinthians 3:12-15).

Although this trial by fire may seem a long way off, don't underestimate its importance. Its results will last for eternity, making our earthly threescore and ten seem like a momentary yawn. Lasting value comes with God's direction.

Plan with Wise Counsel

We are in a war. We can try to fight it alone or we can surround ourselves with other committed soldiers. Consider what Scripture says about counselors.

- Many counselors: *"Without consultation, plans are frustrated, but with many counselors they succeed"* (Proverbs 15:22 NASB).
- Wise counselors: "For by wise guidance you will wage war, and in abundance of counselors there is victory" (Proverbs 24:6 NASB).
- Listen to counsel: *"The way of a fool is right in his own eyes, but a wise man is he who listens to counsel"* (Proverbs 12:15 NASB).

Dedicating Your Workplace to God

Dedicating your workplace to God should be a regular activity. It helps us to be aware of God's presence. In his book *Anointed for Business*, Ed Silvoso has developed an effective method for dedicating, embracing and improving your workplace. The steps are as follows:

Deal with Personal Sin

"Ask the Lord if there is any personal sin that is hindering your anointing in the workplace. Confess any sin God brings to mind. Ask for His grace to turn away from it completely."

It is essential that you examine yourself with transparent honesty. A person of character treats people with respect, is trustworthy, responsible, fair, caring, and a good citizen.

➢ List any personal sins.

Deal with Corporate Sin

"Ask the Lord if there is any corporate sin that is hindering your workplace. Confess any sin God brings to mind. Ask for His grace to turn away from it completely."

Corporate sin may take the form of broken relationships, contracts and agreements; taking advantage of a competitor; unethical practices; unpaid wages; stealing at work. We need to stand in the gap for others by prayerfully interceding for them. We need to recognize and confess sins of others as if they were our own. Pray for conviction, mercy, and forgiveness. Repent and pray for restitution so that all may walk in spiritual freedom. In the Old Testament, Noah, Daniel, and Job were intercessors who stood in the gap.

➢ List any corporate sins.

Dedicate Your Workplace

Ask Jesus to come into your workplace. Ask for His perfect sufficiency to replace your insufficiency. Renew your commitment to do your work God's way. Go to the door, open it and say, "Come in, Jesus. I need you." Walk around your workplace and claim it for the Kingdom. Talk to Jesus about every person with whom you work. Make a commitment to ask the Lord to help you walk with Him daily in your place of work by being aware of His presence.

➤ What day and time will I do this?

➤ Who might I invite to pray with me?

Select a Place at Work to Meet with God

Select a place to meet with God, seeking His wisdom to increase your value and contribution to the workplace.

➤ Where is my place to meet with God?

Recognize the Father, Son, and Holy Spirit as Head of the Workplace

"Acknowledge the Father as the Chairman of the Board, Jesus as the CEO, and the Holy Spirit as the legal counsel. Proclaim their supreme superiority over you and your workplace." Listen and receive your wisdom from God. Be sensitive to the leading of the Holy Spirit. Pray that the decision makers in your workplace will be led by God.

➤ What might God be saying to me?

Embracing and Improving the Workplace

No matter where you find yourself in the marketplace today, your first essential step is to cultivate the right attitude: Embrace your calling to transform that place through the power of God in you. God is not satisfied with your mere survival in the workplace. He has placed you there to bring transformation.

The Seventy in Luke chapter ten played a role similar to the one God has for you. Consider the four steps they took and how those steps can be repeated in today's workplace. The four steps are blessing, embracing, improving and bringing the Kingdom of God to your workplace.

Bless Your Workplace by Being a Peacemaker

Affirm that your job is God's gift to you. Speak peace into your workplace. Bless those whom you work with each day. Acknowledge the fact that God has placed you there to bring transformation. As you place the interests of others ahead of your own, you stand out and gain influence as a peacemaker. This is how Paul said it to the Philippians.

> *Do nothing out of selfish ambition or vain conceit, but in humility consider others better than yourselves. Each of you should look not only to your own interests, but also to the interests of others. Your attitude should be the same as that of Christ Jesus: Who...made himself nothing, taking the very nature of a servant...humbled himself and became obedient to death—even death on a cross!...for it is God who works in you to will and to act according to his good purpose. Do everything without complaining or arguing, so that you may become blameless and pure, children of God without fault in a crooked and depraved generation, in which you shine like stars in the universe (Philippians 2:3-5, 8, 13-15).*

> ➤ When will I speak peace over my workplace and bless those who work with me?

Embrace Your Workplace through Fellowship

Embrace your workplace by giving your very best effort to your job and to those with whom you are working. Look for ways to strengthen your workplace relationships through God-led fellowship.

Make sure that your actions demonstrate the high value you place on each person.

> What good things can I affirm about my employer and job?
> What relationships can I strengthen, and how will I do it?

Improve Your Workplace through Prayer

Improve your workplace by praying for the felt needs in people's lives. Observe, pray, and meet needs in the workplace, especially those in your circle of influence. Pray for God's grace and strength to act on what He has put on you heart. Nothing points marketplace people toward the Lord more than a demonstration of generous compassion and answered prayer. Don't hesitate to ask God for miracles. You don't have to have (or be) everyone's solution—you are not God. But you *are* His representative. Do what you can, and pray for what you can't do. Intercede on behalf of those in your circle of influence—your neighbors.

> What is one felt need of each person I listed above?
> What is one way I can care for each one (and their needs) other than prayer?

Bring the Kingdom of God to Your Workplace

Affirm that the Kingdom of God is advancing in your workplace because you are blessing it, embracing it, improving it, and bringing the Kingdom of God to it. As God draws near to those you are praying for, let them know that you have been praying for them and that God loves them.

> What transformations do I desire to see in the marketplace?
> What might my workplace look like as the Kingdom of God comes to it? Describe a possible before-and-after version of its mission, vision, values, processes, language, morals and ethics.

For a downloadable copy of "Laying the Foundation for Planning" go to **www.MyStrategicPlan.com/kingdom - under "Books."**

Assessment: For Organizations

Assess your organization from an outside perspective. Observe your organization as an employee, customer, supplier, or competitor. For a downloadable "Assessment for Organizations" go to **www.MyStrategicPlan.com/kingdom - under "Books."**

Reflection and Discussion

1. Discuss each of the four steps in Luke 10 as applied to the workplace: Bless, Embrace, Improve, and Bring the Kingdom of God. What might each step look like for you in your place of work?

2. Share a story of God's power in answer to prayer at your place of work.

3. Pray for a need you presently have, asking God to bring a breakthrough. Consider asking a few others at your place of work to join you in prayer for this need.

CHAPTER 17

PLAN FOR WORKPLACE TRANSFORMATION

May he give you the desire of your heart and make all your
plans succeed.—Psalm 20:4

In the last chapter, we laid the foundation for planning; in this chapter, we provide the template—the various components needed—for you to begin creating your own plan. Keep in mind that this plan relates specifically to transforming your workplace.

The process is as important as the plan itself because it helps you understand your workplace so you can align your unique gifts and God-given resources to take advantage of the opportunities God provides. Your plan will include developing a mission and vision statement, identifying your core values, setting specific goals, and determining a set of actions to achieve those goals.

Three prerequisites for planning:
1. Believe that you can do it.
2. Believe that God wants you to do it.
3. Believe that it will make a difference.

It is important to view your plan as a living, dynamic document. Planning is a process that is ongoing and never-ending, changing as your situation changes and as God directs. If you would like to go beyond this chapter's condensed personal plan for transforming your workplace, you can find additional information on strategic planning at **www.MyStrategicPlan.com, www.MyNonProfitPlan.com, or www.MyChurchPlan.com**. These sites are designed respectively for businesses, nonprofits, and churches.

Remember, a good plan coupled with appropriate action gives you traction to go from where you are to where God wants you to be! For a downloadable "Plan for Workplace Transformation" go to **www. MyStrategicPlan.com/kingdom - under "Books."**

Mission Statement

A mission statement is a statement of purpose. It indicates the primary need you are meeting and the primary means you are using. It should be personal, based on your unique gifts, passions, and sense of calling. It should inspire you, capturing the essence of the highest purpose you wish to serve. It should be concise so you can easily memorize it for instant recall. It must be clear so you can use it to make decisions, letting it help you recognize which opportunities are within the bulls-eye, and which ones—regardless of how attractive they seem—should be left for someone else.

To create a mission statement, you need to understand how God has uniquely gifted you with core strengths, abilities, and gifts. Your uniqueness is not an accident; embrace it and develop your plans around it. With this in mind, your mission statement will express your understanding of God's call on your work, focusing on who you are and what you do.

Creating a mission statement and ordering your life around it is a matter of training to become everything God designed you to be. It is a matter of diligence, wholeheartedly pursuing God's pleasure. *"Do you not know that in a race all the runners run, but only one gets the prize? Run in such a way as to get the prize. Everyone who competes in the games goes into strict training. They do it to get a crown that will not last; but we do it to get a crown that will last forever. Therefore I do not run like a man running aimlessly; I do not fight like a man beating the air. No, I beat my body and make it my slave so that after I have preached to others, I myself will not be disqualified for the prize"* (1 Corinthians 9:24-27).

A proactive, focused person with a refined mission statement is a far more effective steward of God's resources than the merely reactive person, the "man running aimlessly," can ever hope to be.

Questions for Developing a Mission Statement

- What is God's purpose for you in your workplace?
- What do you do well? Look at your matrix of strengths, skills, and spiritual gifts.
- Considering all the needs you see in the marketplace, which ones do you feel most passionate about meeting?
- Where can you really make a difference? Look at the opportunities and specific needs that match your unique qualifications.

> ➢ *Action Item*

Write your mission statement, attempting to use only one sentence.

Vision Statement

A good vision statement is a powerful motivator, providing a clear image of how you want your workplace to look three to five years from now. Envision it, by faith, as though the changes have already occurred. Create a snapshot that you can see and understand at a glance but which implies much more content than it details. For instance, it should at least imply the direction you are headed, the focus you should have, the activities to be pursued, and the capabilities you plan to develop. The power of the vision is the attractiveness of the destination; a compelling destination will motivate you, even in weariness, to press on in spite of setbacks and unfriendly terrain.

A godly vision is based on God's will for your place of work. Vitally connected to God's heart, it pictures the met needs of others. It is God-sized, requiring His power to fulfill. It makes your heart surge, carries you to heights you never dreamed possible, and drives exponential growth. Scripture says, *"Record the vision and inscribe it on tablets, that the one who reads it may run"* (Habakkuk 2:2).

The quest to create an inspiring vision will require imagination and a willingness to step out of your comfort zone. If your God is merely "safe," your strategies, computer models, and long hours of work will ensure no more than your human effort can accomplish. Reading the biographies of people God used greatly in the past will enable you to see the daring, the almost embarrassing audacity that drove them to their knees in dependency. You will begin to ask, Where is that for me? Seek God for it. Every good thing comes as a gift from His hand—even faith.

Visionary leaders are focused and determined in their relentless pursuit of compelling ideas. Consider these examples of visionary leaders.

- Strolling through a Japanese park, an engineer had a passing thought: Wouldn't it be nice to combine rich music with outdoor beauty? He conceived an idea that he later developed into the Walkman.

- William Booth walked through London streets, horrified by the poverty all around him. He and his wife had been searching for a worthwhile life purpose. They discovered it in founding the Salvation Army.

- A fur trader in Labrador fished in sub-zero weather. When his catches froze, he discovered how well they retained their flavor. Clarence Birdseye later pioneered the multi-billion-dollar frozen-food industry.

- David's idea to build God's temple came out of his "holy discontent" with what he had already accomplished. His purpose was to glorify God's name, unite and then expand the Kingdom (1 Chronicles 28). Although God did not allow David to be the temple's builder, He gave him the vision for it and enabled his son Solomon to complete the project.

Questions for Developing a Vision Statement

- How has God been leading you?
- What dreams do you have for your workplace in the next three to five years?
- How do you hope to influence your workplace?
- If you knew you would not fail, what would you do to make a difference?
- Is your vision big enough to require faith?

➢ *Action Item*

Write your vision statement, using one or two sentences.

Core Values

There are hundreds of good values. Sifting through them to discover the handful that are most important to you is rarely a simple process. It is an important process, however, because the resulting core values become a distinctive imprint of your personality and motivation. They become the guiding principles that determine how you will conduct business as you choose to maintain them regardless of the cost.

Questions for Identifying Core Values

- What values and beliefs guide your daily interactions?
- What are the core values and beliefs in your workplace?
- What values will you not sacrifice for anything?

➢ *Action Item*

Write a list of concise values or beliefs that are deeply meaningful to you. Then select three to five values you are most reluctant to surrender. These are your core values.

Goals

Taking your vision and mission from abstract ideals to concrete realities means segmenting an intimidating operation into smaller achievable actions. This requires goals: specific performance targets that define what kind, how much, and by when. In order to meet a goal, you must achieve or exceed all three measurements you have set for yourself. In the absence of those clear measurements, you do not have goals; you have mere wishes.

The art of setting goals is finding the balance between what is faith-stretching and what is presumptuous. Prayerfully seek God's guidance for goals that will stretch you and your organization to full potential.

Questions for Creating Goals

- What large outcomes in your vision should be reduced to achievable steps?
- How can you translate those steps into a series of measurable targets?
- Do all of your goals contain all three measurements?

➢ Action Item
In faith, write specific goals for areas where you can make a difference in your workplace. Check to be sure that each goal is specific, measurable, aggressive yet achievable, relevant, and time specific.

Tactics – Specific Actions

Tactics are specific action steps to implement your goals, a to-do list of necessary responsibilities and deadlines. If you are in a position to delegate, a great method to get buy-in from others is to collaborate with them on goals for each person. Ask them to write out their tactics and be responsible for making sure each one is accomplished en route to the goal.

Questions for Developing Tactics

- What specific actions are required to carry out each goal?
- What can you delegate and to whom?
- What resources do you need to accomplish these goals?

➢ Action Item

Write down a set of specific actions to achieve each goal. Determine the necessary resources and the appropriate personnel. Recruit the personnel, giving them sufficient authority to develop and implement their tactics.

Implementation

To achieve ministry goals, you need a good plan and good implementation. A plan addresses the what and why of activities. Implementation addresses the who, where, when, and how, turning the plan into actions that accomplish your goals and fulfill your vision.

Questions for Implementation

- Dates: What date(s) will you schedule to focus on your ministry plan?
- Goals: What do you want to achieve?
- Measure Results: What is happening?
- Evaluate Performance: Why is it happening?
- Corrective Action: What should you do about it?

➢ *Action Item*

Begin implementing your plan by answering the appropriate questions. Set a date to evaluate your commitments and progress so that you can take corrective action to ensure that the goals are attained.

Reflection and Discussion

1. How would you define vision? What makes Christian vision distinctive?

2. Who is the most visionary leader you know? Tell how this person lives out a sense of vision. How does it affect you?

3. Using no more than one or two sentences, state your current vision for life. Describe the process by which you arrived at this vision.

4. Do you evaluate how well you are doing God's work with the same intensity you use in evaluating your sales, profit, or debt-to-equity ratio?

5. How can you know your vision comes from God? What tests might you apply to help clarify this?

6. Describe why the vision you are pursuing is so important to you. When your vision is fulfilled, what will have changed for you and for others?

7. Complete the "Plan for Workplace Transformation" at **www. MyStrategicPlan.com/kingdom - under "Books."**

REFERENCES

Cope, Landa. *The Old Testament Template: Relearning to Disciple Nations God's Way.* www.OTTemplate.org.

Hammond, Pete. "Ten Ways to Support Ministry in the Workplace." His Church at Work (www.hischurchatwork.com).

Hamon, Bill "The Saints Movement, Excerpts from Dr. Bill Hamon's new book 'The Day of the Saints,'" *Christian Business Today,* 2001, Christian International Business Network, Santa Rosa Beach, FL.

High, David. *Kings & Priests* (Oklahoma City, OK: Books for Children of the World, 1998).

Jacobs, Buck. "The C12 Group: An Action Plan for Ministry." Copyright The C12 Group 2003.

Marshall, Rich. *God@Work – Discovering the Anointing for Business.* (Shippensburg, PA: Destiny Image Publisher, Inc., 2000).

Morgan, Michael. "The Church and Marketplace Ministry – A Mega Mind-shift Necessary." www.churchshift.com.

Novak, Michael. "What is a Calling?" *The Life @ Work Book-Sixteen Respected Leaders Talk About Blending Biblical Wisdom and Business Excellence.* by Editors of *The Life@Work Journal,* Word Publishing: Nashville, 2000.

Packer, James I. - "The Christian's Purpose in Business." Chewning, Richard, Ph.D., by Editor. *Biblical Principles & Business* – The Practice. Navpress: Colorado Springs, 1990.

Peacocke, Dennis. "Co-Managing the Earth: The Foundational Work of the Christian Marketplace Ministry." *Business Reform* Vol.3, No.6, Dec. 2003, p.58.

Ross, West. "How Can Churches Help Those in the Workplace?" His Church at Work (www.hischurchatwork.com).

Russell, Doug. "The Gifts of Business." *Business Reform*, vol. 4, No.3, p. 24-25, 36-37.

Strong, James. *Enhanced Strong's Lexicon* (Logos Research Systems Inc., 1995), anointed (#5548).

Silvoso, Ed. *Anointed for Business* (Ventura: Regal, 2002).

Silvoso, Ed. "The Church was not Born in the Upper Room." His Church at Work. (www.hischurchatwork.com).

Smucker, Jim and Beryle Jantzi. "Can Business and Church be Partners?" His Church at Work. (www.hischurchatwork.com).

The Sentinel Group. *The Quickening*. 2003. www.TransformNations.com.

Transformational Leadership Coaching. Virginia Beach, VA (www.transformationalcoaching.com)

Walker, Ken. "When God Comes to Work," *Advance* Q2:04, Vol.40, No.2: Foursquare World, June 2004.